Discover the Best Jobs For You

By Drs. Ron and Caryl Krannich

DISCOVER THE BEST JOBS FOR YOU

4th Edition

Ronald L. Krannich, Ph.D.
Caryl Rae Krannich, Ph.D.

IMPACT PUBLICATIONS
Manassas Park, VA

Library of Congress Cataloguing-in-Publication Data

Krannich, Ronald L.
    Discover the best jobs for you / Ronald L. Krannich, Caryl Rae Krannich—
4th Edition
       p. cm.
    Includes bibliographical references and index.
    ISBN 1-57023-158-3
    1. Job hunting. 2. Vocational guidance. 3. Vocational interests. I. Krannich,
Caryl Rae. II. Title
    HF5382.K69 2001
    650.14—dc21   00-054160

Publisher: For information on Impact Publications, including current and forthcoming publications, authors, press kits, online bookstore, and submission requirements, visit Impact's website: *www.impactpublications.com*

Publicity/Rights: For information on publicity, author interviews, and subsidiary rights, contact the Media Relations Department: Tel. 703-361-7300, Fax 703-361-7300, or email: *discover@impactpublications.com.*

Sales/Distribution: All bookstore sales are handled through Impact's trade distributor: National Book Network, 15200 NBN Way, Blue Ridge Summit, PA 17214, Tel. 1-800-462-6420. All other sales and distribution inquiries should be directed to the publisher: Sales Department, IMPACT PUBLICATIONS, 9104 Manassas Drive, Suite N, Manassas Park, VA 20111-5211, Tel. 703-361-7300, Fax 703-335-9486, or email: *sales@impactpublications.com*

Contents

Preface

MILLIONS OF PEOPLE EACH YEAR FIND JOBS AND change careers. Some are more successful than others in finding the right job for them. For some, the process is relatively easy and results in rewarding jobs. For others, the process is painful and yields less than satisfactory results.

If you are looking for a job or contemplating a career change, this is a good time to take stock of your interests, values, abilities, skills, and goals **before** writing resumes, responding to job listings, or networking for job information. Unfortunately, many job seekers do last things first and thereby neglect to address the **basics** of the job finding process. This should not happen to you.

This book is all about doing first things first—(1) assessing your interests, values, abilities, and skills; (2) setting career goals and formulating a job objective; and (3) relating this information about yourself to specific jobs **before** going on to other job search steps that ultimately result in job interviews and offers. For the key to job search success lies in yourself—knowing who you are and what you want to do in reference to the world of work. However difficult and time consuming, you simply must answer important questions about yourself before you can communicate your qualifications and aspirations to employers.

We wrote this book because we saw a need to bring together some of the major thinking about careers that would help guide job seekers through the job search maze. Unlike some authors or books, we are not interested in developing, trademarking, or promoting another unique assessment system of questionable validity. There are plenty of these systems available, from pencil-and-paper exercises to computer-generated analyses and profiles, that already populate a rather bewildering career assessment landscape. Most are *"more or less useful,"* depending on your situation and goals. Many generate a momentary *"aha"* effect, but few give useful currency for connecting to the right job or career.

Our goal here is to bring some clarity and direction to a rather fascinating area filled with a variety of "magic pill" exercises and formulas that are often promoted by a new variety of "snake oil" salespeople who claim a client base of users who appear satisfied and successful. In so doing, we identify two different approaches that should assist you in clarifying what it is you do well, what you enjoy doing, and where you want to go. While each approach requires different investments of your time and energy, as well as alternative ways of thinking about yourself, both approaches result in focusing your job search in directions that should prove useful to you. If followed properly, these approaches should put you on the road to finding the right job for you.

Our emphasis throughout this book is on **options**. There are alternative ways to reach the same destination, but you first need a road map that identifies your options before you can decide which way to go. If, for example, you need to better understand your interests and skills and how they relate to different jobs, we outline alternative ways of doing so, from self-directed pencil-and-paper exercises to professionally administered and interpreted tests, computer software programs, and self-scoring online tests. If you feel you need additional assistance, we identify numerous other books, websites, and professional counseling services that can help you. As such, *Discover the Best Jobs For You* should serve as a useful resource for finding what you need in the process of discovering the best jobs for you. It should also help you better define your destination.

We wish you well in your search for your best job. But do yourself a favor: organize your thinking around doing first things first. Become better acquainted with yourself, especially your interests, skills, goals, and accomplishments. Begin your job search by **first** examining who you are and where you want to go. Then take action centered around a clear objective. As you will discover in the following pages, **the single-minded pursuit of an objective may be your greatest asset**—regardless of the method you use for defining your objective. Objectives can make a significant difference in how you select a job or career.

Whatever you do, get organized for what may become the greatest adventure of your life—discovering the best jobs for you!

Ron and Caryl Krannich

Discover the Best Jobs For You

1

Do First Things First

D O YOU LOVE WHAT YOU'RE DOING? IS YOUR LIFE all work and no play, or are you pursuing a life you really love living? Are there other things you would rather do but you're not sure exactly what they are or how to go about doing them? What do you plan to do with the rest of your life? Do you feel you've made the right career choices thus far or do you see other possibilities for your future? What are your career and lifestyle goals?

Love What You Do, Do What You Love

Many people simply love their work. Enthusiastic, motivated, driven, and positive about their future, they believe they have the best job in the world—regardless of the size of their paycheck. They can't wait to get to work on Monday morning, and they gladly put in 10- and 12-hour days. Not surprisingly, they're a special breed of positive-thinking workaholics. Their life revolves around their career and work world. They find their work challenging, satisfying, and fun. Indeed, they wouldn't trade their work for anything; they don't look forward to retirement. They are rewarded in many ways, from the interesting nature of their work to the talented people they work with. Some can't believe their good luck: they even receive generous pay and benefits for something they really love to do! And their career future looks brighter than ever. They feel very fortunate in having such a great job. Retirement is not an attractive concept.

Others are less job-possessed. These people are perhaps best termed "lifeaholics" rather than "workaholics." They especially enjoy their work because it enables them to live the life they love. Most important of all, they have a life that includes quality time with their families as well as time to pursue personal interests and hobbies, contribute to their church and community, and travel to interesting places. They have a satisfying job that gives them the time and financial resources to enjoy several other important elements in what they believe is a satisfying and balanced life. They're looking forward to retirement when they will have even more time to enjoy the life they've come to love, because they have a job that contributes to living the life they love. They are some of the fortunate few who have a life in addition to a wonderful job. Their career perspective is best summarized as *"great job, great life!"*

Nearly 50 percent of Americans say they would make a different career choice today than they made when they first entered the job market – given a choice.

And there are still others who neither enjoy their job nor their life. Many have made bad career choices. They would love to change their job and their life—if only they could. Indeed, nearly 50 percent of Americans say they would make a different career choice today than they made when they first entered the job market—if they had a choice. This does not necessarily mean they are unhappy with their current work. Rather, it means they might be happier had they made different career choices when they were young and inexperienced. They might be happier in a different career that also enabled them to pursue a different lifestyle.

Finding Your Best Job

Are you one of these fortunate few who has found a job you really love, one that fits well and has become your best job? If not, this book is for you. For as we outline in subsequent chapters, discovering the best jobs for you involves a process of becoming better acquainted with yourself. It requires relating what you do well and enjoy doing to different jobs that best fit your particular motivations and behavioral patterns.

How do people find their best jobs? What is it they do that others don't? Are they more intelligent than others? Do they have extraordinary education, training, and experience? Perhaps they know the right people. Or maybe their timing is right, or they are just lucky.

The best jobs go to those who create their own luck. They know who they are, what they want, and where they are going. They have clear goals, keep focused on those goals, and make intelligent moves within the job market. They understand themselves, the job market, and employers. They know how to identify the right employers as well as how to best communicate their qualifications to employers. Most important of all, they know which jobs are best for them.

Get Ready For Your Future

Most adults spend between 35 and 60 hours a week in work-related activities. Some greet the Monday morning alarm clock with excitement and anticipation. Others dread the start of a new work week. Which are you or which will you become?

What do you want to do next month, next year, or even the rest of your life? Do you want a job that leads to major career advancement, more money, and greater power, or do you prefer less responsibility, less stress, and a slower pace? Perhaps you are primarily interested in pursuing a particular lifestyle centered around skills you most enjoy using. Do you want to work for someone else or run your own show? Do you require lots of independence or do your work best in team settings? Where do you see your career and lifestyle five, ten, or twenty years from now?

These questions lie at the heart of discovering the best jobs for you. They are the subject of this book. More important, they should become your central concerns as you develop a well organized and coherent plan for job and career success.

Find the Best Jobs

Many people end up in the wrong jobs because they fail to plan their careers around their major strengths and motivations, and because they look for jobs in all the wrong places and for all the wrong reasons. Not knowing what they do well and enjoy doing, they stumble into jobs by accident, or they primarily seek jobs they think might offer good salaries, excellent benefits, and a promising future. They're forever trying to acquire one of those "best" or "hottest" jobs that are periodically announced by the media as having a great future for those who get on today's bandwagon. They seldom view jobs as being right for them. They fail to relate jobs to their long-term patterns of interests, skills, and abilities. Once on the job, they may discover the job is an inappropriate "fit" for their abilities and motivational patterns. Salary and benefits become secondary considerations as they find few on-the-job rewards. The compensation may be good but the work does not bring out the best in them. Unhappy with the inappropriate fit, they start job hunting again with the hope that "this time" they may find the right job for renewed career success.

Few people are lucky enough to find jobs and pursue careers they really love. This is not to say most people are unhappy with their present jobs. Contrary to what many writers tell us—that nearly 80 percent of the workforce are unhappy with their jobs—annual surveys continue to confirm that nearly 80 percent of today's workforce are relatively content with their present jobs. But could many of these people do much better if they used a different approach to finding jobs and advancing their careers?

> *The secret to discovering the best jobs for you is much more than an external search for "where the jobs are."*

Concerned with either keeping their present jobs or just finding one to pay the bills, most people seldom focus on the larger question of what jobs are really right for them. Instead, when looking for employment, they look **outside** themselves by focusing on "where the jobs are." This approach leads them on a search for job vacancy announcements that look interesting to them rather than for jobs that may be right for them. They become preoccupied with fitting into the requirements of different jobs rather than trying to find jobs that are fit for them.

The secret to discovering the best jobs for you is much more than an external search for "where the jobs are." It goes beyond the major initial approach of job seekers—to quickly put together a resume so they can respond to vacancy announcements. While finding vacancy announcements and writing resumes are important elements in a job search, they should not be the first steps. They are not even the second or third things you need to do. They are intermediate activities conducted later in a job search.

At the very minimum, finding the best jobs for you begins with **you**—knowing your interests, values, abilities, skills, motivations, and dreams. You must analyze, synthesize, and reformulate this self-assessment information into a powerful **objective**. This objective, in turn, provides the foundation for a well organized job search that will ultimately link your strengths and goals to the needs of employers.

Your first task should be to look inside yourself. Become better acquainted with yourself by discovering where you've been in the past, where you are at present, and where you wish to go in the future. By initially focusing on your interests, skills, and abilities—rather than alternative job vacancies you feel you might be able to fit into—you begin building a sound basis for giving yourself positive career direction for many years to come.

This book is all about doing first things first. And the first thing you need to do is answer the most important questions relating to your interests, values, abilities, skills, and objectives. In other words, you need to identify what it is you do well and enjoy doing **prior to** identifying where the jobs are and how to get one. The pages that follow show you how to best do this as you put yourself on a sound road to long-term career success.

Discover a Job "Fit" For You

Our major concern is that you find a job that is fit for you rather than one you think you might be able to fit into. This is an important distinction central to the remaining chapters in this book. Trying to "fit into a job" is the typical way most people find jobs. They look

You should find a job that is fit for you rather than one to fit into.

for job vacancies and then try to stretch their qualifications in order get the job. While some people find jobs they enjoy by using this approach, others are less fortunate. They often discover they are in the wrong job.

On the other hand, finding a job "fit for you" is what this book is all about. Our approach is based on a great deal of experience and common sense regarding how to best find and keep a job as well as advance a career. Time and again job seekers discover it is more important to know what they want to do than to know where the job vacancies can be found. It's essential to know what you do well (**abilities and skills**), what you enjoy doing (**interests and values**), and what you want to do (**objective**) before writing each section of your resume or going for a job interview. If you do these first things first, you are more likely to find a job fit for you rather than one you may or may not fit into very well.

Get Organized For Success

Doing first things first, throughout this book we stress the importance of assessing your interests, abilities, and skills and formulating these into a powerful objective that will help guide you to the right job. This is not a book on *"What are the jobs?"* or *"Where are the jobs?"* or even *"How do I get a job?"* You will find numerous such books that primarily list alternative jobs and careers. Some of the best such books are identified in our bibliography (Chapter 15) and in the order form at the end of this book. A few books attempt to identify the 100+ "hottest" jobs and careers for the coming decade, including our own *Best Jobs For the 21st Century*. Others are primarily directories of the most widely available jobs today. And still others attempt to show readers how to get into a few of today's best paying jobs.

> *Armed with this self knowledge, you will be in the best position to know what particular jobs and careers you should pursue.*

We focus on the important **linkage** between you and alternative jobs. Our approach begins and ends with you in reference to the job market. While you eventually need to research alternative jobs and careers (Chapter 12) as well as survey job vacancies, you first need to do what we outline in the first eleven chapters—discover what you do well and enjoy doing and what you want to do in the years ahead. Armed with this self knowledge, you will be in the best position to know what particular jobs and careers you should pursue. You will know that while some jobs may look interesting, they are inappropriate for your particular mix of interests and abilities. You will save a great deal of time and effort, avoid future disappointments, and enjoy what you will be doing in the future if you read this book prior to going on to finding a specific job you think might be good for you.

The chapters that follow are designed to easily walk you through the process of self-discovery. After examining alternative jobs and careers in Chapter 2 and your job search skills in Chapter 3, we examine different approaches to finding a job in Chapter 4. We conclude with advice on organizing a job search around the notion of doing "first things first." Chapter 4 is the critical overview chapter that shows you how all the job search pieces fit together as you face the task of organizing each step of your job search.

The remaining chapters take you step-by-step through the process of identifying your pattern of interests, values, abilities, skills, and motivations and then formulating them into a powerful job objective that will give your job search the necessary direction for success. Central to these chapters are two very different approaches to career direction.

Deterministic/Predestination Approach

The first approach is widely practiced by a particular group of career counselors who believe in the power of predestination, the magic of testing, and the predictive power of probability. Many come from pastoral counseling backgrounds that continue to direct their thinking about career choices and behavior. This approach is clearly articulated by Richard Bolles (*What Color Is Your Parachute?*, *Three Boxes of Life*, and *The New Quick Job Hunting Map*) and Arthur Miller and Ralph Mattson (*The Truth About You*) and espoused by a legion of career counselors raised on the approaches of these popular writers/

> *This approach takes you down a narrow and somewhat pessimistic road where you are advised to be "realistic" about your future.*

practitioners/gurus. Basic to this approach is both a deterministic and probabilistic theory of individual behavior—your future performance will most likely be a repeat performance of your past patterns of behavior. Major proponents justify using this approach on explicit religious grounds: since God has put his imprint on you and you cannot escape your fate, you need to discover what he has pre-ordained for you. The approach ostensibly uncovers God's vision for you in the form of a "career map." Much of their work is based on the pioneering work of Haldane and Crystal (see Germann and Arnold's *Bernard Haldane*

Associates Job and Career Building, and Barkley and Sandburg's *The Crystal-Barkley Guide to Taking Charge of Your Career*).

This deterministic/predestination approach takes you down a narrow and often pessimistic road where you are advised to be "realistic" about your future. An analysis of historical data on you—rather than information on your future aspirations—should determine where you will go in the future. By discovering your past patterns of motivated abilities and skills, you will be able to formulate realistic career goals as well as an appropriate job search action plan.

Despite claims of effectiveness, doses of religious fundamentalism, and some hocus-pocus, most self-assessment devices using this deterministic approach are designed to reconstruct your past "patterns" of work behavior. Related to this approach is a personality "type" theory based on the work of psychologist Carl Jung and developed into testing applications by the mother/daughter team of Katherine Briggs and Isabel Briggs Myers (Myers-Briggs Type Indicator™) and recently popularized by Paul D. Tieger and Barbara Barron-Tieger in *Do What You Are* (New York: Little, Brown) and Jean Kummerow, Linda Kirby, and Nancy Barger in *WORKTypes* (New York: Warner). Similar to the determinism underlying the much overworked interests, skills, abilities, and values approach, this personality type approach views personality as a blueprint. In its simplest form, this approach assures individuals that if they know and recognize their personality type, they should be better able to find their perfect job or career, one that is conducive to their particular personality type. As such, this is still a deterministic approach—you can't escape your past personality patterns that ostensibly translate into future on-the-job personality and behavioral patterns.

Other career writers develop similar typologies and classification systems using psychological indicators and interest and value inventories for describing, explaining, predicting, and prescribing career choices. Creating intellectually interesting classification systems for better understanding how individuals choose careers and behave in the workplace (description and explanation), they often confuse their analytical constructs with reality and then make a critical and unwarranted leap into predicting and prescribing career choices for individuals. Such classification systems take on a life and reality of their own when they move from description and explanation to prediction and prescription. A recent example of such an intellectual exercise involving a unique classification system that goes on to prescribe career choices is Martin Yate's "professional competencies" and "personal preferences" approach (*Beat the Odds* and *CareerSmarts: Jobs With a Future*. At best an interesting exercise, it, too, fits into our deterministic/predestination category of approaches.

Whether working with interests, skills, abilities, values, or personality as predictors of career choices, career satisfaction, or even job performance, each of these deterministic/predestination approaches basically takes you down that same sobering path which actually becomes a hall of mirrors—you are what you are; you'll be what you have already been regardless of your dreams and goals. We identify many of the most popular such approaches and their assessment devices and critique both their strengths and weaknesses.

Self-Transformation Approach

The second approach is widely used in business—primarily sales and entrepreneurship—and in some religious circles. This is a self-help psychological approach centered around such notions as "self-transformation," "thinking big," "following your dreams," "positive thinking," "you can be anything you want to be," and "reach for the stars." It's the basic motivational approach used in such direct-sales operations as Amway, Shaklee, and Tupperware, as well as in real estate and insurance; the popular wealth-building approaches based on the self-motivational philosophies of Napolean Hill (*Think and Grow Rich*), Maxwell Maltz (*Psycho-Cybernetics*), David Schwartz (*The Magic of Thinking Big*), Claude Bristol (*The Magic of Believing*), Anthony Robbins (*Personal Power, Unlimited Power, and Awaken the Giant Within*), Zig Ziglar (*How to Get What You Want*), Og Mandino (*Secrets of Success*), Wayne W. Dyer (*Manifest Your Destiny*), and many others; and the secular-religious writings of Dr. Robert H. Schuller (*You Can Become the Person You Want to Be* and *If It's Going to Be, It's Up to Me*), Dr. Norman Vincent Peale (*The Power of Positive Thinking*), and Rabbi Harold Kushner (*When All You've Ever Wanted Isn't Enough*). This is the stuff of motivational speakers who arouse members of their audience to transform their lives through positive thinking. Practitioners of this approach do not dwell on history, predictable patterns of past behavior, or analytical constructs that are best left in the college classroom. Indeed, one's history and past patterns of behavior are often seen as the **problem** rather the solution for charting a new future. These self-help philosophers see the past as an impediment—something people need to break away from as they transform themselves and head in new directions. Being "realistic" is not a major concern, because realism is most likely a function of one's past patterns of behavior which are blinders to the future. These approaches stress the importance of setting high level—even unrealistic—**goals** and then developing the power to stay highly motivated and focused on those goals. Being single-mindedly focused on pursuing big goals is the basis for breaking out of past patterns as individuals embark on a new and hopefully brighter future.

The language of this approach is radically different from the other approach. The self-transformation approach focuses on **goals, motivation, action, and drive**—key elements largely absent in the language of the deterministic/predestination practitioners. Indeed, the almost total absence of this language in the other approach raises serious questions of whether or not those practitioners are dealing with real people who are capable of taking action and making changes in their behavior. They call into question the validity of their simple classification systems and complicated testing devices that are supposed to inductively provide "objective" answers to important career questions.

> *The first approach is conservative, deterministic, probabilistic, and realistic. The second approach is radical, risky, and refreshing.*

What, for example, is the difference between their advice and that of the psychic? Is one approach merely inductive while the other is basically deductive—but both use a series of procedures to arrive at equally valid, or invalid, conclusions? One wonders if there is much of a difference in actual outcomes! In fact, practitioners of both approaches appear to achieve very similar outcomes as evidenced by their many anecdotal cases of success.

At first glance these are radically different approaches that can produce very different outcomes for you. The first approach used by most career counselors is conservative, deterministic, probabilistic, and realistic. The second approach is radical, risky, and refreshing. Both face a fundamental dilemma when dealing with the future:

> *How can you chart your future if it is merely a reflection of your past personality and behavior, or if it is based on a great deal of unrealistic big thinking?*

The chapters that follow show how both approaches can best work for you. Each has certain strengths and weaknesses, and each works well for different people, depending on how they wish to chart their future. For some, the deterministic/predestination approach provides an excellent map for clarifying goals and organizing a well-focused job search centering around one's major strengths. For others, who are interested in making major changes in their behavior, this approach is too limiting. We outline how they can best make changes without becoming captives of their pasts or frustrated by an inability to attain their aspirations.

Where Do You Go From Here?

We wish you well as you take this journey into the wild and sometimes confusing world of self-discovery. While we are primarily concerned at this stage in taking you through the most critical initial stages of a job search, we also recognize the need to continue on through other important stages that result in meeting potential employers and receiving job offers. These other steps are outlined in several of our other books: *Change Your Job, Change Your Life; High Impact Resumes and Letters; Dynamite Resumes; Dynamite Cover Letters; 201 Dynamite Job Search Letters; The Savvy Resume Writer; Savvy Interviewing; 101 Dynamite Answers to Interview Questions; Interview For Success; Dynamite Tele-Search; Dynamite Networking For Dynamite Jobs;* and *Dynamite Salary Negotiations.*

This book is primarily concerned with identifying what you do best and enjoy doing in relation to today's job market. Each year millions of job hunters turn to career planning books for assistance. Many begin with a general book and next turn to resume and interview books. Others begin with a resume book and later seek other types of job re-sources, including letter writing and networking books. Some go directly to software programs or visit various websites for producing resumes and preparing for job interviews.

If this book represents your first career planning book, you may want to supplement it with a few other key resources. Many of them are available in your local library and bookstore or they can be ordered directly from Impact Publications (see the "Career Resources" section at the end of this book, pages 194-195). Most of these resources, along with hundreds of others, are available through Impact's comprehensive "Career Superstore" on the Internet:

www.impactpublications.com

This website contains almost every important career and job finding resource available today, including many titles that are difficult if not impossible to find in bookstores and libraries. You will find everything from additional self-assessment books to books on resume writing, interviewing, government and international jobs, military, women, minorities, students, entrepreneurs as well as videos and software programs. This is an excellent resource for keeping in touch with the major resources that can assist you with every stage of your job search as well as with your future career development plans. Impact's site also includes new titles, specials, and job search tips for keeping you in touch with the latest in career information and resources. You also can request a free copy of their abbreviated career catalog (4-page flier) by sending a self-addressed stamped envelope (#10 business size). Send your request to:

IMPACT PUBLICATIONS
ATTN: Free Career Flier
9104 Manassas Drive, Suite N
Manassas Park, VA 20111-5211

Discover the Best Jobs For You

The following pages are designed to assist you in developing an effective job search that will lead to discovering the best jobs for you. It addresses the **fundamentals** for getting yourself organized and focused on what it is you need to do to get that job. If you follow our advice, do first things first, and implement with persistence, you can join thousands of others who have learned the secrets to discovering their best jobs today and in the decade ahead!

2

Identify the Best Jobs
For Tomorrow

ARE THE BEST JOBS FOR YOU ALSO FOUND AMONG
the best jobs predicted for the future? Let's put your
concerns within the larger context of future job trends
before we turn to you, the individual, who needs to identify
which jobs are *really* best for you. The best jobs for you
hopefully will also be among the 100 best jobs predicted for the coming
decade. Based on certain assumptions about the economy, these are
some of the fastest growing jobs that should generate millions of job
opportunities. Many are good jobs that offer excellent salaries and
advancement opportunities. They will be some of the most sought-after
jobs in the future.

This chapter in no way should imply that the best jobs for you will
be found among the so-called "hot" jobs for the coming decade. Indeed,
the best jobs for you will most likely be discovered through an
examination of your interests, skills, and abilities in relation to
alternative jobs and careers—the job that best "fits" you.

What Are the Jobs?

Where are the jobs, and *how* do I get one? These are the first two
questions most people ask when seeking employment. But one other
equally important question should precede these traditional questions:

"*What* are the jobs of tomorrow?"

For the nature of jobs is changing rapidly in response to (1) technological innovations, (2) the development and application of technology to the workplace, and (3) the demand for a greater variety of consumer goods and services in a booming economy. Many of today's savvy job seekers need answers to "what," "where," and "how" questions for the coming decade.

Jobs in the year 2010 will look very different from those in 2000. Indeed, if we project present trends into the future and believe what futurists tell us about emerging new careers, the coming decade will offer unprecedented job and career opportunities.

But such changes and opportunities have costs. The change in jobs and occupations will be so rapid that skills learned today may become obsolete in another five to ten years. Therefore, knowing what the jobs are becomes a prerequisite to knowing how to prepare for them, find them, and change them in the future.

Beware of Changing Occupational Profiles

A few words of caution are in order on how you should and should not use the information in this chapter. If you wish to identify a growing career field to plan a career, do so only after you identify your interests, skills, and abilities—the subjects of Chapters 7, 8, and 9. You need to determine if you have the proper skills or the aptitude and interests to acquire the necessary skills. The next step is to acquire the training before conducting a job search. Only then should you seriously consider pursuing what appears to be a growing field.

If you wish to identify a growing career field to plan a career, do so only after you identify your interests, skills, and abilities.

At the same time, you should be aware that the statistics and projections on growing industrial and occupational fields may be inaccurate. First, they are based on traditional models and economic studies conducted by the U.S. Department of Labor, Bureau of Labor Statistics. Unlike fortune tellers and soothsayers who communicate in another world and many futurists who engage in "informed flights of fancy" and "brainstorming," the Bureau conducts "empirical studies" which assume a steady rate of economic growth—no major ups or downs. Such occupational projections are nothing more than "best guesses" based upon a traditional model which assumes continual, linear growth. This planning model does not deal well with the reality of cyclical changes, as evidenced by its failures during the turbulent 1980s and 1990s when boom-and-bust cycles, coupled with the emergence of unique events and crises, invalidated many of the Bureau's forecasts. For example, the U.S. Department of Labor projected a high unemployment rate of 7.6 percent for 1982; but in that year unemployment stood at 10.8 percent. In addition, a deepening recession and government program cuts brought on by a series of international crises, domestic economic failures, and ideological changes were unanticipated developments which resulted in the actual decline in public employment for the first time since World War II. Thus, in 1982 there were 316,000 fewer public employees than in the year before!

> *By the year 2000, the "new economy" had become a talent-driven economy. Recruitment and retention were central issues for most employers.*

The 1990s witnessed similar unexpected economic growth and decline. Federal government cutbacks, low inflation, and unprecedented growth of businesses and the stock market helped create an expected economic boom that saw federal government employment decline by nearly 400,000 and overall unemployment drop to 4.8 percent in 1997—the lowest in more than two decades. In an economy where 6 percent unemployment is considered full employment, the economy of the second half of the 1990s experienced major labor shortages, especially in high-tech industries and services. The slow growth predicted for the 1990s was anything but slow after 1995.

By the year 2000, the U.S. had experienced one of its longest periods of sustained economic growth as the economy continued to boom. It was accompanied by an unprecedented unemployment rate of 3.8 percent and continuing labor shortages in several high-tech fields. The so-called "new economy" had been transformed into a talent-driven economy in which recruitment and retention were central issues for most employers. How to find and keep talented workers become the number one priority in many companies. Individuals with the right combination of skills and experience had no problem finding well paying jobs which also came with generous benefits. In the new talent-driven economy, skilled workers were highly valued. The decade ahead may well provide us with more unique economic scenarios which produce similar unpredictable outcomes, from major recessions to economic booms.

Second, during a period of turbulent change, occupational profiles may become quickly outdated. Training requirements change, and thus individuals encounter greater uncertainty in career choices. For example, based on trend analyses, many people believe that promising careers lie ahead for computer programmers. This may be true if thousands of newly trained individuals do not glut the job market with obsolete computer programming skills. Physicians, who once faced promising careers, now enter a very different job market dominated by HMOs and insurance companies which have significantly altered the role of physician and made this once glamorous profession less attractive than a decade or two ago.

A similar situation arises for students pursuing the much glamorized MBA and law degrees. As more MBAs graduate and glut the job market, the glitter surrounding this degree may diminish, especially if the economy experiences a downturn. While the demand for lawyers increased substantially during the past decade and a large number of students continue to enroll in law schools, competition for legal positions has been keen during the past few years as more and more law graduates flooded a shrinking job market. Opportunities for lawyers may not increase much in the decade ahead. The demand for lawyers may actually decline due to substantial restructuring of the legal profession as lawyers become more competitive, promote more efficient legal services, hire more paralegals, change fee and billing practices, introduce more technology to traditional legal tasks, and develop more do-it-yourself legal approaches; as the criminal justice system under-goes restructuring; and as Americans become less litigious due to the high costs of pursuing legal action.

Expect Job Growth in Most Occupations

The growth in jobs has been steady during the past three to four decades. From 1955 to 1980, for example, the number of jobs increased from 68.7 to 105.6 million. This represented an average annual increase of about 1.5 million new jobs. During the 1970s the number of jobs increased by over 2 million per year. And between the years 1983 and 1994 the number of jobs increased by 24.6 million, a strong growth rate of 24 percent over an 11-year period or over 2 million new jobs each year. The number of jobs is expected to increase from 141 million in 1998 to 171 million in 2008, representing a 14 percent increase or 2 million new jobs each year.

Job growth during the 1990s slowed but remained steady at about 1.5 million new jobs each year. The slowdown reflected demographic changes in society. By the year 2008 the labor force should consist of 154.6 million workers—up 12 percent or by 17 million from 1998. This increase is nearly the same as in the previous 10-year period—1988 to 1998—when the civilian workforce increased by 13 percent.

Highlighting these patterns of job growth are 16 forecasts, based on U.S. Department of Labor data and projections and other recent analyses, which represent the confluence of demographic, economic, and technological changes in society:

1. **Growth of the labor force slows while the number of jobs increases—a formula for continuing labor shortages.**

    The growth in the labor force will slow to 154.6 million by the year 2008—a 12 percent increase over the 138 million figure in 1998. This represents half the rate of increase during the previous 15-year period; it reflects an overall slow population growth, with a near-zero population birthrate of 0.7 percent per year. At the same time, the number of jobs is expect to increase by 20 million—from 141 million in 1998 to 161 million in 2008.

2. **The labor force will be racially and ethnically more diverse.**

    The racial and ethnic mix of the work force in the year 2008 will be even more diverse than today, given the differential birth and immigration rates of various racial and ethnic groups. Blacks, Hispanics, Asians, and other minority groups will represent 29.3 percent of the work force in the year 2008—up from 26.1 percent in 1998. These groups also will account for 35 percent of labor force entrants.

Hispanics, Asians, and other minorities will increase at a faster rate than blacks and white non-Hispanics.

3. **More young people will begin entering the job market in larger numbers.**

The number of 16 to 24 year-olds entering the job market will slightly increase from 1998 to 2008. Representing 16 percent of the labor force, this age group will actually grow more rapidly than the rest of the work force, the first time this has happened in over 25 years. The largest group of workers, ages 25 to 44, will decline from 51 percent of the labor force in 1998 to 44 percent of the labor force in 2008. Regardless of the slight increase in young people entering the labor force, there still be a shortage of such workers for entry-level positions. Businesses depending on this age group for students, recruits, customers, and part-time workers—especially colleges, the Armed Forces, eating and drinking establishments, and retail stores—must draw from a small pool of young people. Competition among young people for entry-level jobs will not be very keen.

4. **The work force will continue to gray as it becomes older.**

As the baby-boom generation becomes more middle-aged, the number of workers 45 and older is expected to increase from 33 to 40 percent of the labor force from 1998 to 2008. The number of older workers, aged 55 years and above, will grow faster than the labor force as a whole.

5. **Women's share of the workforce will continue to increase incrementally.**

Women will represent over half of all entrants into the labor force in the decade ahead. While accounting for 39 percent of the labor force in 1972 and 46.3 percent of the labor force in 1998, women in the year 2008 are projected to constitute 47.5 percent of the labor force. By the year 2008, 4 out of 5 women ages 25-54 will be in the labor force.

6. **Education requirements for most new jobs will rise.**

Most new jobs will require strong basic education skills, such as reading, writing, oral communication, and computation. Over one-third of all new jobs will require at least a bachelor's degree; nearly all of the 50 highest paying occupations require a college degree. Many of these jobs will include important high-tech components which will require previous specialized education and training as well as the demonstrated ability to learn and acquire nontraditional education and training to continuously re-tool skills.

7. **The fastest growing occupations will be in executive, managerial, professional, and technical fields—all requiring the highest levels of education and skill.**

Three-quarters of the fastest growing occupational groups will be executive, administrative, and managerial; professional specialty; and technicians and related support occupations—occupations that require the highest levels of education and skill. Few opportunities will be available for high school dropouts or those who cannot read or follow directions. A combination of greater emphasis on productivity in the workplace, increased automation, technological advances, innovations, changes in consumer demands, and import substitutions will decrease the need for workers with little formal education and few skills—helpers, laborers, assemblers, and machine operators.

8. **Employment will increase for most occupations.**

As the population continues to grow and become more middle-aged and affluent, demands for more services will increase accordingly. Except in the cases of agriculture, mining, and traditional manufacturing, the coming decade will be a period of steady to significant job growth in all occupations. While 20 million new jobs will be added to the U.S. economy between 1998 and 2008, these jobs will be unevenly distributed across major industrial and occupational groups due to the continuing restructuring of the economy and the increased education and training requirements for most jobs.

9. **The greatest growth in jobs will take place in service industries and occupations.**

   Over 95 percent of all new jobs in the decade ahead will be in the service-producing industries with services such as business (personnel supply, computer, data processing), health care, and professional and miscellaneous services leading the way. The number of jobs in services is expected to rise by over 50 percent between 1998 and 2008, adding 11.8 million new jobs to the work force. Health care and business will be the fastest growing services during this period. Professional and miscellaneous services, such as management, public relations, research, and testing, will also exhibit strong growth. Jobs in computer and data processing services are expected to grow the fastest—by 117 percent, from 1998 to 2008.

10. **Transportation, public utilities, finance, insurance, real estate, and wholesale and retail trade industries will grow at very similar rates—13 to 15 percent—from 1998 to 2008.**

    Employment in transportation and utilities is expected to increase by 674,000 jobs, or 14 percent. Employment in finance, insurance, and real estate should increase by 960,000 jobs, or 13 percent. Employment in wholesale and retail trade should increase by 7 and 14 percent respectively, adding nearly 7 million new jobs.

11. **Federal government employment will decline but state and local government employment will increase at different rates for different levels of government as well as for governments in different regions of the country.**

    Employment in government, including public education and public hospitals, is expected to increase by over 9 percent,

from 19.8 to 21.7 million jobs. Federal government employment is expected to further decline by 165,000 jobs. This
continuing decline reflects the overall strategy to contract
out government services, downsize federal agencies, elimin-
ate programs, and decentralize federal functions to state and
local governments. Except during recessionary periods, state
and local government employment will increase by 1 to 2
percent each year, with local governments in the rapidly
developing and relatively affluent cities and counties of the
West and Southwest experiencing the largest employment
growth rates.

12. **Employment growth in education at all levels will be
    incremental.**

    Employment in both public and private education will
    increase slightly at all levels due to projected population and
    enrollment increases. Job opportunities should increase for
    teachers, teacher aides, counselors, and administrative staff.
    Many schools and universities will experience continuing
    shortages of teachers and faculty members in technical
    fields, especially in computer science and information
    technology.

13. **Jobs in manufacturing will decline somewhat in the
    decade ahead.**

    From 1998 to 2008, manufacturing jobs are expected to
    decline by 1 percent, from the 1998 level of 18.8 million.
    Most of the decline will affect production jobs. These
    declines will be due to productivity gains achieved through
    improved production methods, advances in technology, and
    increased trade.

14. **Employment in agriculture, forestry, and fishing is
    expected to increase in the decade ahead; employment in
    mining will continue to decline.**

    Employment in agriculture, forestry, and fishing is expected
    to increase by nearly 5 percent, from 2.2 to 2.3 million. The

strongest growth will take place in agricultural services, offsetting expected employment declines in crops and livestock. Employment in mining will continue to decline, by 19 percent from 590,000 to 475,000 jobs, due to labor-saving machinery and increased imports.

15. **Glamorous new occupations, responding to new technological developments and consumer demands, will offer exciting new opportunities for job seekers who are well educated and skilled in the jobs of tomorrow.**

    New occupations, created through a combination of technological innovations and new service demands, will provide excellent career opportunities for those who possess the necessary skills and drive to succeed in the decade ahead. New occupational terms, such as *cyberian*, will enter our occupational vocabulary during the coming decade.

16. **The hottest career fields will be in science, engineering, computer technology, and health care services.**

    Look for these jobs to be the highest-demand and highest-paying jobs in the coming decade: biological scientist, physician, mechanical engineer, chemical engineer, computer scientist, computer engineer, materials engineer, and medical technologist. Demand also will be high for these less well-paid jobs: special education teachers, personal and home care aides, home health aides, and physical therapists.

Examine Growing and Declining Occupations

The Department of Labor divides occupations into 16 broad groups based on the Standard Occupational Classification, which is used by all government agencies for collecting occupational information:

- Executive, administrative, and managerial occupations
- Engineers, scientists, and related occupations
- Social science, social service, and related occupations

- Teachers, librarians, and counselors
- Health-related occupations
- Writers, artists, and entertainers
- Technologists and technicians
- Marketing and sales occupations
- Administrative support occupations, including clerical
- Service occupations
- Agricultural and forestry occupations
- Mechanics and repairers
- Construction occupations
- Production occupations
- Transportation and material moving occupations
- Handlers, equipment cleaners, helpers, and laborers

Every two years the department's Bureau of Labor Statistics updates its employment outlook for the coming decade and publishes the results in the November issue of the *Monthly Labor Review* as well as the latest edition of the biannual ***Occupational Outlook Handbook***. For the latest statistics and projections relating to several tables presented in this chapter, please visit the website of the Bureau of Labor Statistics: ***http://stats.bls.gov***. You also can access online the complete text of the popular ***Occupational Outlook Handbook***: ***http://stats.bls.gov./oco home.htm***.

Assuming a moderate rate of economic growth in the decade ahead —not boom-and-bust cycles—the U.S. Department of Labor in 1997 projected an average growth rate of 14 percent for all occupations. Technical and service occupations will grow the fastest:

Projected Employment Changes, 1996-2006

Occupational group	Total increase/decrease in new jobs	Percentage change
All occupations	18,574,000	+14.0
■ Professional specialty	4,826,000	+26.6
■ Services	3,853,000	+22.2
■ Executive, administrative, managerial	2,324,000	+17.2
■ Marketing and sales	2,264,000	+15.5
■ Administrative support, clerical	1,806,000	+18.1
■ Operators, fabricators, laborers	1,522,000	+8.5
■ Precision production, craft, repair	1,002,000	+6.9
■ Technicians and related support	940,000	+20.4
■ Agriculture, forestry, fishing, and related	37,000	+1.0

The top ten industries with the fastest employment growth include the following:

Top 10 Industries With Fastest Employment Growth, 1996-2006
(in thousands)

Industry description	Employment Change, 1996-2006			
	1996	2006	Number	Percent
■ Computer and data processing services	1,208	2,509	1,301	108
■ Health services	1,172	1,968	796	68
■ Management and public relations	873	1,400	527	60
■ Miscellaneous transportation services	204	327	123	60
■ Residential care	672	1,070	398	59
■ Personnel supply services	2,646	4,039	1,393	53
■ Water and sanitation	231	349	118	51
■ Individual and miscellaneous social ser.	846	1,266	420	50
■ Offices of health practitioners	2,751	4.046	1,295	47
■ Amusement and recreation services	1,109	1,565	457	41

While job growth is expected in most occupations in the coming decade, the following 30 occupations will grow at the fastest percentage rate, contributing nearly 3.7 million new jobs. Occupations contributing the largest job growth in terms of the actual number of new jobs generated will be in service industries requiring a wide range of skills. Nearly half of the 30 fastest growing occupations will be in the health services alone. Most of these fast growing occupations require a Bachelor's degree or some form of moderate- to long-term postsecondary training.

Fastest Growing Occupations, 1996-2006
(in thousands)

Occupation	Number of New Jobs Created	Percentage Change
■ Database administrators, computer support specialists, and all other computer specialists**	249,000	118
■ Computer engineers**	235,000	109
■ Systems analysts**	520,000	103
■ Personal and home care aides	171,000	85

- Physical and corrective therapy
  assistants and aides   66,000   79
- Home health aides   378,000   76
- Medical assistants   166,000   74
- Desktop publishing specialists   22,000   74
- Physical therapists**   81,000   71
- Occupational therapy assistants and aides   11,000   69
- Paralegals*   76,000   68
- Occupational therapists**   38,000   66
- Teachers, special education**   241,000   59
- Human services workers   98,000   55
- Data processing equipment repairers   42,000   52
- Medical records technicians*   44,000   51
- Speech-language pathologists and
  audiologists***   44,000   51
- Dental hygienists   64,000   48
- Amusement and recreation attendants   138,000   48
- Physician assistants**   30,000   47
- Respiratory therapists*   37,000   46
- Adjustment clerks   186,000   46
- Engineering, science, and computer
  systems managers**   155,000   45
- Emergency medical technicians   67,000   45
- Manicurists   19,000   45
- Bill and account collectors   112,000   42
- Residential counselors*   74,000   41
- Instructors and coaches, sports and
  physical training   123,000   41
- Dental assistants   77,000   38
- Securities and financial services
  sales workers   100,000   38

* Requires Associate's degree
** Requires Bachelor's degree
*** Requires Master's degree

The Department of Labor projects the following occupations will have the largest job growth:

Occupations With Largest Projected Job Growth, 1996-2006

Occupation	Employment Change		Best Training Source
	Number	Percent	
■ Cashiers	530,000	17	Short-term on-the-job
■ Systems analysts	520,000	103	Bachelor's degree
■ General managers and top executives	467,000	15	Work experience plus bachelor's or higher degree

■ Registered nurses	411,000	21	Associate's degree
■ Salespersons, retail	408,000	10	Short-term on-the-job training
■ Truck drivers	404,000	15	Short-term on-the-job training
■ Home health aides	378,000	76	Short-term on-the-job training
■ Teacher aides and educational assistants	370,000	38	Short-term on-the-job training
■ Nursing aides, orderlies and attendants	333,000	25	Short-term on-the-job training
■ Receptionists and information clerks	318,000	30	Short-term on-the-job training
■ Teachers, secondary	312,000	22	Bachelor's degree
■ Child care workers	299,000	36	Short-term on-the-job training
■ Clerical supervisors and managers	262,000	19	Work experience in a related occupation
■ Database administrators, computer support specialists, and all other computer scientists	249,000	118	Bachelor's degree
■ Marketing and sales worker supervisors	246,000	11	Work experience in related occupation
■ Maintenance repairers, general utility	246,000	18	Long-term on-the-job training
■ Food counter, fountain related workers	243,000	14	Short-term on-the-job training
■ Teachers, special education	241,000	59	Bachelor's degree
■ Computer engineers	235,000	109	Bachelor's degree
■ Food preparation workers	234,000	19	Short-term on-the-job training
■ Hand packers and packagers	222,000	23	Short-term on-the-job training
■ Guards	221,000	23	Short-term on-the-job training
■ General office clerks	215,000	7	Short-term on-the-job training
■ Waiters and waitresses	206,000	11	Short-term on-the-job training
■ Social workers	188,000	32	Bachelor's degree

■ Adjustment clerks	183,000	46	Short-term on-the-job training
■ Cooks, short order and fast food	174,000	22	Short-term on-the-job training
■ Personal and home care aides	171,000	85	Short-term on-the-job training
■ Food service and lodging managers	168,000	28	Work experience in a related occupation
■ Medical assistants	166,000	74	Moderate-term on-the-job training

The importance of education and training in future occupational growth is highlighted with the following Department of Labor projections:

Fastest Growing Occupations By Level of Education and Training, 1996-2006

Fastest Growing Occupations	Occupations with largest numerical increase in employment
First-professional degree	
■ Chiropractors ■ Veterinarians & veterinary inspectors ■ Physicians ■ Lawyers ■ Clergy	■ Lawyers ■ Physicians ■ Clergy ■ Veterinarians & veterinary inspectors ■ Dentists

Fastest Growing	Largest numerical increase
Doctoral degree	
■ Biological scientists ■ Medical scientists ■ College and university faculty ■ Mathematicians and all other mathematical scientists	■ College & university faculty ■ Biological scientists ■ Mathematicians and all other mathematical scientists
Master's degree	
■ Speech-language pathologists and audiologists ■ Counselors ■ Curators, archivists, museum technicians	■ Speech-language pathologists and audiologists ■ Counselors ■ Psychologists ■ Librarians, professional

- Psychologists
- Operations research analysts

- Operations research analysts

Work experience plus bachelor's or higher degree

- Engineering, science, and computer systems managers
- Marketing, advertising, and public relations managers
- Artists and commercial artists
- Management analysts
- Financial managers

- General managers and top executives
- Engineering, science, and computer systems managers
- Financial managers
- Marketing, advertising, and public relations managers
- Artists and commercial artists

Bachelor's degree

- Database administrators computer support specialists
- Computer engineers
- Systems analysts
- Physical therapists
- Occupational therapists

- Teachers, secondary school
- Database administrators and computer support specialists
- Teachers, special education
- Computer engineers

Associate degree

- Paralegals
- Health information technicians
- Dental hygienists
- Respiratory therapists
- Cardiology technologists

- Registered nurses
- Paralegals
- Dental hygienists
- Radiological technologists and technicians
- Health information technicians

Fastest Growing	Largest numerical increase

Postsecondary vocational training

- Data processing equipment repairers
- Emergency medical technicians
- Manicurists
- Surgical technologists
- Medical secretaries

- Licensed practical nurses
- Automotive mechanics
- Emergency medical technicians
- Hairdressers, hairstylists, and cosmetologists

Work experience in a related occupation

- Food service and lodging managers
- Teachers and instructors, vocational education and training
- Lawn service managers
- Instructors, adult education
- Nursery and greenhouse managers

- Clerical supervisors and managers
- Marketing and sales worker supervisors
- Teachers and instructors, vocational education and training
- Instructors, adult (nonvocational) educational

Long-term training and experience (more than 12 months of on-the-job training)

- Desktop publishing specialists
- Flight attendants
- Musicians
- Correction officers
- Producers, directors, actors, and entertainers
- Maintenance repairers, general utility
- Cooks, restaurant
- Corrections officers
- Musicians
- Police patrol officers

Moderate-term training and experience (1 to 12 months of combined on-the-job training)

- Physical and corrective therapy assistants and aides
- Medical assistants
- Occupational therapy assistants
- Social and human services assistants
- Instructors and coaches, sports and physical training
- Medical assistants
- Instructors and coaches, sports and physical training
- Social and human services assistants
- Dental assistants
- Physical and corrective therapy assistants

Short-term training and experience (up to 1 month of on-the-job experience)

- Personal and home care aides
- Home health aides
- Amusement and recreation attendants
- Adjustment clerks
- Cashiers
- Salespersons, retail
- Truck drivers, light and heavy
- Home health aides

Determine "The Best" Jobs For You

The fastest growing occupational fields are not necessarily the best ones to enter. The best job and career for you will depend on your particular

> *The best job and career for you will depend on your particular mix of skills, interests, and work and lifestyle values.*

mix of skills, interests, and work and lifestyle values. Money, for example, is only one of many determiners of whether or not a job/ career is particularly desirable. A job may pay a great deal of money, but it also may be very stressful and insecure, or it is found in an undesirable location. "The best" job for you will be one you find very rewarding in terms of your own criteria and priorities.

Periodically some observers of the labor market attempt to identify what are the best, the worst, the hottest, the most lucrative, or the most promising jobs and careers of the decade.

One of the most ambitious attempts to assemble a list of "the best" jobs in America is presented in Les Krantz's *Jobs Rated Almanac*. Similar in methodology to *Places Rated Almanac* for identifying the best places to live in America, this book evaluates and ranks 250 jobs in terms of six primary "job quality" criteria: income, stress, physical demands, environment, outlook, and security. According to this analysis, the 20 highest ranking ("best") jobs by accumulated score of these criteria are:

"The Best" Jobs in America

Job Title	Overall rank	Overall score
▪ Website manager	1	103
▪ Actuary	2	126
▪ Computer systems analyst	3	129
▪ Software engineer	4	179
▪ Mathematician	5	203
▪ Computer programmer	6	216
▪ Accountant	7	278
▪ Industrial designer	8	298
▪ Hospital administrator	9	307
▪ Web developer	10	307
▪ Paralegal assistant	11	324
▪ Parole officer	12	342
▪ Meteorologist	13	344
▪ Technical writer	14	344
▪ Medical secretary	15	349
▪ Medical technologist	16	362
▪ Financial planner	17	364
▪ Medical laboratory technician	18	365
▪ Astronomer	19	371
▪ Historian	20	377

The 20 worst jobs, or those that rank at the very bottom of the list of 250, include the following:

"The Worst" Jobs in America

Job Title	Overall rank	Overall score
■ Roustabout	250	1403
■ Lumberjack	249	1375
■ Fisherman	248	1340
■ Construction worker (laborer)	247	1326
■ Cowboy	246	1310
■ Dancer	245	1286
■ Sheet metal worker	244	1247
■ Taxi driver	243	1245
■ Roofer	242	1243
■ Seaman	241	1239
■ Garbage collector	240	1208
■ Automobile painter	239	1194
■ Boilermaker	238	1162
■ Carpenter	237	1161
■ Meter reader	236	1157
■ Stevedore	235	1156
■ Ironworker	234	1156
■ Farmer	233	1152
■ Bricklayer	232	1152
■ Construction machinery operator	231	1148

For the relative rankings of all 250 jobs as well as the ratings of each job on individual criterion, consult the latest edition of the *Jobs Rated Almanac*, which should be available in your local library or bookstore.

One of the most recent (2001) examinations of the best jobs in the decade ahead—those offering high pay, fast growth, and the most new jobs—is found in Ferguson's *25 Jobs That Have It All* (Chicago, IL: Ferguson Publishing Co.). They identify these 25 jobs as the top ones:

- ■ Advertising Account Executives
- ■ College Professors
- ■ Commodities Brokers
- ■ Computer Network Administrators
- ■ Computer Programmers
- ■ Computer Systems/Programmer Analysts
- ■ Database Specialists
- ■ Electrical and Electronics Engineers

- Financial Services Brokers
- Graphic Designers
- Hardware Engineers
- Health Care Managers
- Illustrators
- Management Analysts and Consultants
- Paralegals
- Physicians
- Police Officers
- Registered Nurses
- Secondary School Teachers
- Social Workers
- Software Designers
- Software Engineers
- Special Education Teachers
- Technical Support Specialists
- Writers and Editors

Look For Exciting New Occupations in the Future

In the early 1980s the auto and related industries—steel, rubber, glass, aluminum, railroads and auto dealers—accounted for one-fifth of all employment in the United States. Today that percentage continues to decline as service occupations further dominate America's occupational structure.

New occupations for the decade ahead will center around information, energy, high-tech, health care, and financial industries. They promise to create a new occupational structure and vocabulary relating to computers, the Internet, robotics, biotechnology, lasers, and fiber optics. By 1999, for example, the Internet reportedly was responsible for 1.3 million new jobs within a four-year period that generated more than $300 billion in business. And as these fields begin to apply new technologies to developing new innovations, they in turn will generate other new occupations in the 21st century. While most new occupations are not major growth fields—because they do not initially generate a large number of new jobs—they will present individuals with fascinating new opportunities to become leaders in pioneering new fields and industries.

Futurists agree that most new occupations in the coming decade will have two dominant characteristics:

- **They will generate fewer new jobs** in comparison to the overall growth of jobs in hundreds of more traditional service fields, such as sales workers, office clerks, truck drivers, and janitors.

- **They require a high level of education and skills** for entry into the fields as well as continuing training and retraining as each field transforms itself into additional growth fields.

If you plan to pursue an emerging occupation, expect to first acquire highly specialized skills which may require years of higher education and training.

Consider the Implications of Future Trends For You

Most growth industries and occupations require skills training and experience. Moving into one of these fields will require knowledge of job qualifications, the nature of the work, and sources of employment. Fortunately, the U.S. Department of Labor publishes several useful sources of information available in most libraries to help you. These include the *O*NET Dictionary of Occupational Titles*, which identifies over 1,100 job titles (reduced from 13,000 titles found in the old *Dictionary of Occupational Titles*). The *Occupational Outlook Handbook* provides an overview of current labor market conditions and projections, as well as discusses nearly 250 occupations that account for 107 million jobs, or 87 percent of the nation's total jobs, according to several useful informational categories: nature of work; working conditions; employment; training, other qualifications, and achievement; job outlook; earnings; related occupations; and sources of additional information.

During the past five years, the U.S. Department of Labor has overhauled its traditional job classification system, which is based on an analysis of the U.S. job market of the 1960s, 1970s, and 1980s. This system had generated over 13,000 job titles as outlined in the *Dictionary of Occupational Titles* and numerous related publications. Known as the O*NET project (The Occupational Information Network), this new occupational classification system more accurately reflects the structure of today's new job market; it condenses the 13,000+ job titles into over 1,100 job titles. The new system is being gradually introduced into career education and it will soon replace the job classification system that has defined most jobs in the U.S. during the past four decades.

Anyone seeking to enter the job market or change careers should initially consult the U.S. Department of Labor publications as well as access information on the new O*NET. The Department of Labor only makes this data available on CD-ROM and online: *www.doleta.gov/ programs/onet*. However, a commercial version of this system, published in book form, is available. You should be able to find it in your local library. If not, the *O*NET Dictionary of Occupational Titles* can be ordered from Impact Publications by completing the form at the end of this book or by going online: *www.impactpublications.com*.

However, remember that labor market statistics are for industries and occupations *as a whole.* They tell you little about the shift in employment emphasis *within the industry,* and nothing about the outlook of particular jobs for you, *the individual.* For example, employment in agriculture was projected to decline by 14 percent between 1985 and 2000, but the decline consisted of an important shift in employment emphasis within the industry: there would be 500,000 fewer self-employed workers but 150,000 more wage and salary earners in the service end of agriculture. The employment statistics also assume a steady state of economic growth with consumers having more and more disposable income to stimulate a wide variety of service and trade industries.

Therefore, be careful in how you interpret and use this information in making your own job and career decisions. If, for example, you want to become a college teacher, and the data tells you there will be a 10 percent decline in this occupation during the next 10 years, this does not mean you could not find employment, as well as advance, in this field. It merely means that, on the whole, competition may be keen for these jobs, and that future advancement and mobility in this occupation may not be very good—on the whole. At the same time, there may be numerous job opportunities available in a declining occupational field as many individuals abandon the field for more attractive occupations. In fact, you may do much better in this declining occupation than in a growing field depending on your interests, motivations, abilities, job search savvy, and level of competition. And if the decade ahead experiences more boom-and-bust cycles, expect most of these U.S. Department of Labor statistics and projections to be invalid for the economic realities of this decade.

Use this industrial and occupational data to expand your awareness of various job and career options. By no means should you make critical education, training, and occupational choices based upon this information alone. Such choices require additional types of information—subjects of the next six chapters—about you, the individual. If identified and used properly, this information will help clarify exactly which jobs are best for you.

3

Test Your Careering Competencies

DOING FIRST THINGS FIRST REQUIRES SOME BASIC self-knowledge about your capabilities to conduct an effective job search. Do you, for example, know what your major strengths are and how to communicate them to potential employers? Do you know which jobs are ideally suited for your particular skills and motivations? Can you develop a one- to two-page resume that clearly communicates your qualifications to employers? How well can you plan and implement a job search that will lead to several interviews and a job offer that is right for you?

We need to first address these questions prior to examining your interests, values, abilities, skills, motivations, and goals.

Careering Competencies

Knowing where the jobs are is important to your job search. But knowing how to find a job is even more important. Before you acquire names, addresses, and phone numbers of potential employers, you should possess the necessary job search knowledge and skills for gathering and using job information effectively.

Answers to many of your job related questions are found by examining your present level of job search knowledge and skills. Successful job seekers, for example, use a great deal of information as well as specific skills and strategies for getting the jobs they want.

Let's begin by testing for the level of job search information, skills, and strategies you currently possess as well as those you need to develop and improve. You can easily identify your level of job search competence by completing the exercise on pages 38-39.

Adding It Up

After you finish this exercise, calculate your overall careering competencies by adding the numbers you circled for a composite score. If your total is more than 75 points, you need to work on developing your careering skills. How you scored each item will indicate to what degree you need to work on improving specific job search skills. If your score is under 50 points, you are well on your way toward job search success. In either case, this book should help you better focus your job search as well as identify job search skills you need to acquire or strengthen.

Your Careering Competencies

INSTRUCTIONS: Respond to each statement by circling which number at the right best represents your situation.

SCALE: 1 = strongly agree   4 = disagree
2 = agree   5 = strongly disagree
3 = maybe, not certain

1. I know what motivates me to excel at work.   1 2 3 4 5

2. I can identify my strongest abilities and skills.   1 2 3 4 5

3. I have seven major achievements that clarify a pattern of interests and abilities that are relevant to my job and career.   1 2 3 4 5

4. I know what I both like and dislike in work.   1 2 3 4 5

5. I know what I want to do during the next 10 years.   1 2 3 4 5

6. I have a well defined career objective that focuses my job search on particular organizations and employers.   1 2 3 4 5

7. I know what skills I can offer employers in different occupations.   1 2 3 4 5

8. I know what skills employers most seek in candidates.   1 2 3 4 5

9. I can clearly explain to employers what I do well and enjoy doing.   1 2 3 4 5

10. I can specify why employers should hire me.   1 2 3 4 5

11. I can gain the support of family and friends for making a job or career change.   1 2 3 4 5

12. I can find 10 to 20 hours a week to conduct a part-time job search.   1 2 3 4 5

13. I have the financial ability to sustain a three-month job search.   1 2 3 4 5

14. I can conduct library and Internet research
    on different occupations, employers,
    organizations, and communities.   1 2 3 4 5

15. I can write different types of effective
    resumes and job search/thank you letters.   1 2 3 4 5

16. I can produce and distribute resumes and
    letters to the right people.   1 2 3 4 5

17. I can list my major accomplishments in
    action terms.   1 2 3 4 5

18. I can identify and target employers I
    want to interview.   1 2 3 4 5

19. I can develop a job referral network.   1 2 3 4 5

20. I can persuade others to join in forming
    a job search support group.   1 2 3 4 5

21. I can prospect for job leads.   1 2 3 4 5

22. I can use the telephone and email to develop
    prospects and get referrals and interviews.   1 2 3 4 5

23. I can plan and implement an effective
    direct-mail and Internet job search campaign.   1 2 3 4 5

24. I can generate one job interview for every
    10 job search contacts I make.   1 2 3 4 5

25. I can follow up on job interviews.   1 2 3 4 5

26. I can negotiate a salary 10-20% above
    what an employer initially offers.   1 2 3 4 5

27. I can persuade an employer to renegotiate
    my salary after six months on the job.   1 2 3 4 5

28. I can create a position for myself
    in an organization.   1 2 3 4 5

TOTAL _____

4

Get Organized
For Success

HOW DO YOU GO ABOUT FINDING YOUR BEST JOB? Do you send resumes in response to vacancy announcements and classified ads? Do you contact employment firms and headhunters? Or do you get on the telephone and make lots of cold calls to potential employers as well as network with friends and colleagues? Perhaps you're technologically savvy and thus prefer spending most of your time looking for a job on the Internet.

Join us as we outline an approach that works well for thousands of successful job seekers each year. Our approach is based upon the notion of **empowerment**—you have within you the power to achieve your career goals. But you must do first things first before initiating the most important steps in your job search.

An Empowerment Process

Finding your best job requires that you (1) know who you are, (2) where you want to go, and (3) how to get there. This involves an important process of moving from an initial stage of self-awareness to several other action stages involving specific job search activities that eventually result in employment.

If you have a clear understanding of each element and relationship within this process, you should be in a better position to know who you are and where you want to go. By relating each element, the process becomes a crucial blueprint revealing how to get where you want to go.

Find Jobs and Change Careers

If you are looking for your first job, re-entering the job market after a lengthy absence, or planning a job or career change, you will join an army of millions of individuals who do so each year. Indeed, between 15 and 20 million people find themselves unemployed each year. Millions of others try to increase their satisfaction within the workplace as well as advance their careers by looking for alternative jobs and careers. If you are like most other Americans, you will make more than 10 job changes and between three and five career changes during your lifetime. If you are under age 30, you may have already held more than 10 different jobs!

Most people make job or career transitions by accident or attribute their job to serendipity and good luck. They do little other than take advantage of opportunities that may arise unexpectedly. While chance and luck do play important roles in finding employment, we recommend that you plan for future job changes so that you will experience even greater degrees of chance and luck!

If you seek comprehensive, accurate, and timely job information, the job market will frustrate you.

Finding a job or changing a career in a systematic and well-planned manner is hard yet rewarding work. The task should first be based upon a clear understanding of the key ingredients that define jobs and careers. Starting with this understanding, you should next convert key concepts into action steps for implementing your job search.

A career is a series of related jobs which have common skill, interest, and motivational bases. You may change jobs several times without changing careers. But once you change skills, interests, and motivations, you change careers.

It's not easy to find a job given the present structure of the job market. You will find the job market to be relatively disorganized, although it projects an outward appearance of coherence, especially in the case of Internet employment sites which give the false appearance of a functioning "job market." If you seek comprehensive, accurate, and timely job information, the job market will frustrate you with its poor communication. While you will find many employment services ready to assist you, such services tend to be fragmented and their performance is often disappointing. Job search methods are controversial and many are ineffective.

No system is organized to give people jobs. At best you will encounter a *decentralized and fragmented advertising system* consisting of job listings in newspapers, trade journals, employment offices, Internet employment sites, or computerized job databanks—all designed to link potential candidates with available job openings. Many people will try to sell you job information, as well as questionable job search services, with the idea that they have exclusive access to certain types of jobs and with false promises of performance. While major efforts continue to create a government-sponsored nationwide computerized job bank (America's Job Bank), which would list available job vacancies on a daily basis, don't expect such a system to soon solve the job information problem. Many of the listed jobs may be nonexistent, or at a low skill and salary level, or represent only some employers. In the end, most systems organized to help you find a job do not provide the information you need in order to land a job that is most related to your skills and interests.

Understand the Career Development Process

Finding a job is both an art and a science; it encompasses a variety of basic facts, principles, and skills which can be learned but which also must be adapted to individual situations. Thus, *learning how to find a job* can be as important to career success as *knowing how to perform a job.* Indeed, job finding skills are often as important to career success as job performance or work-content skills. Without effective job search skills, you may have difficulty locating jobs and communicating your qualifications to employers.

> *Job finding skills are often as important to career success as job performance or work-content skills.*

Our understanding of how to find jobs and change careers is illustrated on pages 43 and 44. As outlined on page 43, you should involve yourself in a four-step career development process as you prepare to move from one job to another.

The Career Development Process

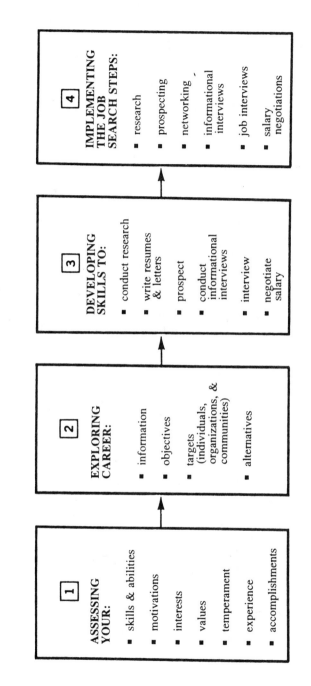

1 ASSESSING YOUR:
- skills & abilities
- motivations
- interests
- values
- temperament
- experience
- accomplishments

2 EXPLORING CAREER:
- information
- objectives
- targets (individuals, organizations, & communities)
- alternatives

3 DEVELOPING SKILLS TO:
- conduct research
- write resumes & letters
- prospect
- conduct informational interviews
- interview
- negotiate salary

4 IMPLEMENTING THE JOB SEARCH STEPS:
- research
- prospecting
- networking
- informational interviews
- job interviews
- salary negotiations

Job Search Steps

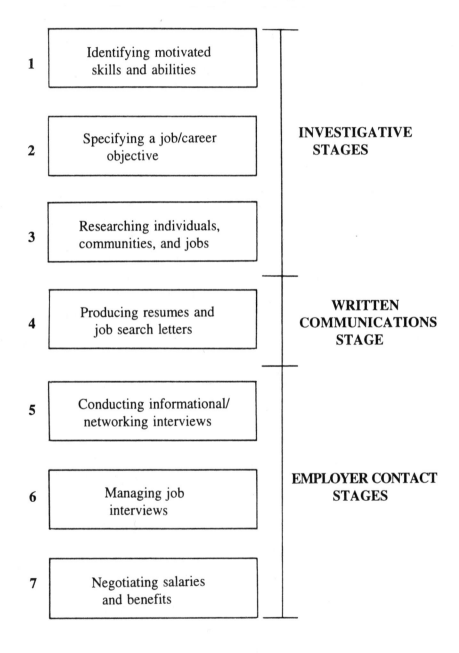

1. **Conduct a self-assessment:**

   This first step involves assessing your skills, abilities, motivations, interests, values, temperaments, experience, and accomplishments—the major concern of this book. Your basic strategy is to develop a firm foundation of information on *yourself* before proceeding to other stages. This self-assessment develops the necessary self-awareness for effectively communicating your qualifications to employers as well as focusing and building your career.

2. **Gather career and job information:**

   Closely related to the first step, this second step is an exploratory, research phase of your career development. Here you need to formulate goals, gather information about alternative jobs and careers through reading and talking to informed people, and then narrow your alternatives to specific jobs.

3. **Develop job search skills:**

   The third step focuses your career around specific job search skills for landing the job you want. As further outlined on page 44, these job search skills are closely related to one another as a series of *job search steps.* They involve conducting research, writing resumes and letters, prospecting and networking, conducting informational interviews, interviewing for a job, and negotiating salary and terms of employment. Each of these job search skills involves well-defined strategies and tactics you must learn in order to be effective in the job market.

4. **Implement each job search step:**

   The final career development step emphasizes the importance of transforming understanding into *action.* You do this by implementing each job search step which already incorporates the knowledge, skills, and abilities you acquired in Steps 1, 2, and 3.

Organize and Sequence Your Job Search

The figure on page 44 further expands our career development process by examining the key elements in a successful job search. It consists of a seven-step process which relates your past, present, and future. We cover all of these steps in subsequent chapters, which deal with skills assessment, research, resume writing, networking, interviewing, and salary negotiations.

Based on this concept, *your past* is well integrated into the process of finding a job or changing your career. Therefore, you should feel comfortable conducting your job search: it represents the best of what you are in terms of your past and present accomplishments as these relate to your present and future goals. If you base your job search on this process concept, you will communicate your *best self* to employers as well as focus on *your strengths* both during the job search and on the job.

Since the individual job search steps are interrelated, they should be followed in sequence. If you fail to properly complete the initial self-assessment steps, your job search may become haphazard, aimless, and costly. For example, you should never write a resume (Step 3) before first conducting an assessment of your skills (Step 1) and identifying your objective (Step 2). Relating Step 1 to Step 2 is especially critical to the successful implementation of all other job search steps. You *must* complete Steps 1 and 2 *before* continuing on to the other steps. Steps 3 to 6 may be conducted simultaneously because they complement and reinforce one another.

Try to sequence your job search as close to these steps, as possible as indicated in the figure on page 48, which outlines a hypothetical job search over a six-month period. The true value of this sequencing will become very apparent as you implement your plan. We'll return to this model job search when we discuss job search planning in Chapter 13.

The processes and steps identified on pages 43 and 44 represent the career development and job search processes used successfully by thousands of job-seekers during the past 50 years. Despite today's changing job market and digital job search techniques, these processes are equally applicable for the decade ahead as long as you recognize the importance of acquiring work-content skills along with job search skills.

You must do much more than just know how to find a job. In the job markets of today and tomorrow, you need to constantly review your work-content skills to make sure they are appropriate for the changing job market. Assuming you have the necessary work-content skills, you should be ready to target your skills on particular jobs and careers that you do well and enjoy doing. You will be able to avoid the trap of trying to fit into jobs that are not conducive to your particular mix of interests, abilities, skills, and motivations.

Organization of Job Search Activities

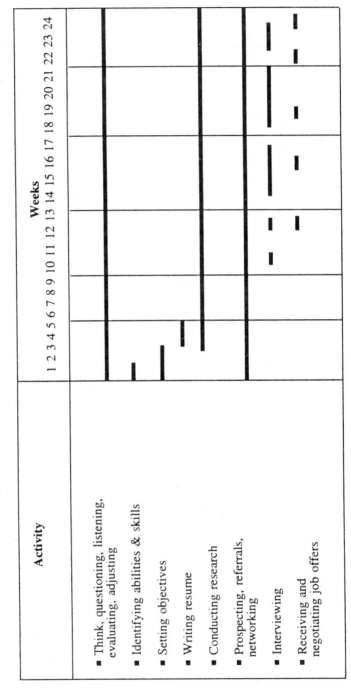

5

Seek Professional Assistance When Necessary

W
HILE SOME PEOPLE CAN SUCCESSFULLY CON-
duct a job search based on the advice of books such as
this, many others also need the assistance of various
professional groups that offer specific career planning and
job search services. These groups provide everything from testing and
assessment services to writing resumes and offering contacts with
potential employers, including job vacancy information and temporary
employment services. Some do one-on-one career counseling while
others sponsor one- to three-day workshops or six- to twelve-week
courses on the various steps in the career planning process. You should
know something about these services before you invest your time and
money beyond this and other career planning and job search books.

Options and Potential Pitfalls

You have two options in organizing your job search. First, you can
follow the principles and advice outlined in this and many other self-
directed books or distilled from content found on several Internet
employment sites. Just read the materials and then put them into
practice by following the step-by-step instructions. Second, you may
wish to seek professional help to either supplement or replace this book.
Indeed, many people will read parts of this book—perhaps all of it—and

do nothing. Unwilling to take initiative, lacking sufficient time or motivation, or failing to follow through, many people will eventually seek professional help to organize and implement their job search. They will pay good money to get someone else to tell them to follow the advice found in this book. Some people need this expensive motivation in order to bring organization and discipline to their job search.

At the same time, we recognize the value of professional assistance. Especially with the critical assessment and objective-setting steps (Chapters 7, 8, and 9), some individuals may need more assistance than our advice and exercises provide. You may, for example, want to take a battery of tests to better understand your interests and values in relation to alternative jobs and careers. And still others, due to a combination of job loss, failed relationships, or depression, may need therapy best provided by a trained psychologist or psychiatrist rather than career testing and information services provided by career counselors. If any of these situations pertain to you, by all means seek professional help.

> **While many services are excellent, other services are useless.**

You also should beware of pitfalls in seeking professional advice. While many services are excellent, other services are useless and fraudulent. Remember, career planning and job assistance are big businesses involving millions of dollars each year. Many people enter these businesses without expertise. Professional certification in these areas is extremely weak to non-existent in some states. Indeed, many so-called "professionals" are self-appointed experts; they get into the business because they are unemployed. In other words, they major in their own problem! Others are frauds and hucksters who prey on vulnerable and naive people who feel they need a "specialist" or "expert" to get them a job. They will take your money in exchange for promises. You will find several services promising to assist you in finding all types of jobs. You should know something about these professional services before you venture beyond this book.

If you are interested in exploring the services of job specialists, begin by looking in the Yellow Pages of your telephone directory or searching on the Internet by entering these keywords: Management Consultants, Employment, Resumes, Career Planning, and Social Services. Also, contact your local community college or various community services groups, including churches, for referrals to such professionals.

You'll find several career planning and employment services, ranging from highly generalized to very specific services. Most services claim they can help you. If you read this book, you will be in a better position to seek out appropriate services as well as ask the right questions for screening such services. You may even discover you know more about finding a job than many of the so-called professionals!

Alternative Employment Services

At least 11 different career planning and employment services provide job search assistance. Each has certain advantages and disadvantages. Approach them with caution. Never sign a contract before you read the fine print, get a second opinion, and talk to former clients about the *results* they achieved through the service. With these words of caution in mind, let's take a look at the variety of services available.

1. Public employment services

Public employment services usually consist of a state agency which provides employment assistance as well as dispenses unemployment compensation benefits. Employment assistance largely consists of job listings and counseling services. However, counseling services often screen individuals for employers who list with the public employment agency. If you are looking for an entry-level job in the $15,000 to $35,000 range, contact this service. Most employers still do not list with this service, especially for positions paying more than $35,000 a year. Although one of the main purposes of these offices is to dispense unemployment benefits, don't overlook these offices because of past stereotypes. Many of these offices have literally "reinvented" themselves for today's new job market by shedding their unemployment, low-wage, and office-of-last-resort images. Many of them offer useful employment services, including self-assessment and job search workshops as well as electronic job banks that match skills and experience with available job vacancies. Many of these offices are now linked to America's Job Bank (*www.ajb.com*), an electronic database which includes job listings throughout the U.S. and abroad. If you are a veteran, you will find many of the jobs listed with state employment offices are designated for veterans. See for yourself if your state employment office offers useful services. You may be pleasantly surprised with both the extent and quality of employment services offered by these offices.

2. Private employment agencies

Private employment agencies work for money, either from applicants or employers. Approximately 8,000 such agencies operate
nationwide. Many are highly specialized in technical, scientific, and
financial fields. The majority of these firms serve the interests of
employers since employers—not applicants—represent repeat
business. While employers normally pay the placement fee, many
agencies charge applicants 10 to 15 percent of their first year salary.
These firms have one major advantage: job leads which you may
have difficulty uncovering elsewhere. Especially for highly specialized fields, a good firm can be extremely helpful. The major
disadvantages are that they can be costly and the quality of the firms
varies. In fact, much of the information acquired through these firms
is now available over the Internet for free, especially through niche
employment sites. Be careful in how you deal with these groups.
Make sure you understand the fee structure and what they will do
for you before you sign anything.

3. Temporary employment firms

During the past decade temporary employment firms have come of
age as more and more employers turn to them for recruitment assistance. In fact, between three to four percent of today's workforce is
classified as "temporary workers." Many of these workers find their
jobs via temporary employment firms. These firms offer a variety
of employment services to both applicants and employers who are
either looking for temporary work and workers or who want to
better screen applicants and employers. Many of these firms recruit
individuals for a wide range of positions and skill levels as well as
full-time employment. If you are interested in "testing the job
waters," you may want to contact these firms for information on
their services. Employers—not job seekers—pay for these services.

4. College/university placement offices

College and university placement offices provide in-house career
planning services for graduating students. While some give
assistance to alumni, don't expect too much help if you have already
graduated. Many of these offices are understaffed or provide only

rudimentary services, such as maintaining a career planning library, coordinating on-campus interviews for graduating seniors, and conducting workshops on how to write resumes and conduct job interviews. Others provide a full range of well supported services including testing and one-on-one counseling. In fact, your best resource may be your local junior or community college. Many of these educational institutions offer career assessment and related employment services to members of the community on a walk-in basis. You can use their libraries and computerized career assessment programs, take personality and interest inventories, or attend special workshops or full-semester career planning courses which will take you through each step of the career planning and job search processes. Many administer two of the most important assessment devises—the _Myers-Briggs Type Indicator®_ and _Strong Interest Inventory_—for nominal fees ($15 versus $100 through a private counseling group). You are well advised to enroll in such a course since it is likely to provide just enough structure and content to assess your motivated abilities and skills and to assist you in implementing a successful job search plan. Check with your local campus to see what services you might use.

5. Private career management and job search firms

Private career and job search firms help individuals acquire job search skills. They do not find you a job. In other words, they teach you much—maybe more but possibly less—of what is outlined in this book. Expect to pay anywhere from $1,500 to $10,000 for this service. If you need a structured environment for conducting your job search, including a private career coach to help you complete each step in the job search process, by all means contract with one of these firms. One of the oldest and most popular firms is Bernard Haldane Associates. Many of their pioneering career planning and job search methods are the basis for modern career counseling and are incorporated in this book. You will find branches of this firm in over 90 cities in the U.S., Canada, and the United Kingdom by visiting their website (_www.jobhunting.com_) or by consulting one of their job search books, such as _**Haldane's Best Resumes For Professionals**_, _**Haldane's Best Cover Letters For Professionals**_, _**Haldane's Best Answers to Tough Interview Questions**_, and _**Haldane's Best Salary Tips For Professionals**_ (Impact Publications).

6. Executive search firms and headhunters

Executive search firms work for employers in finding employees to fill critical positions in the $60,000+ salary range. They also are called "headhunters," "management consultants," and "executive recruiters." These firms play an important role in linking high level technical and managerial talent to organizations. Don't expect to contract for these services. Executive recruiters work for employers—not applicants. If a friend or relative is in this business or you have relevant skills of interest to these firms, let them know you are available—and ask for their advice. On the other hand, you may want to contact firms that specialize in recruiting individuals with your skill specialty. Several books identify how you can best approach "headhunters" on your own: *Headhunters Revealed! Career Secrets For Choosing and Using Professional Recruiters* (Darrell W. Gurney), *How to Select and Use an Executive Search Firm* (A. R. Taylor); *How to Answer a Headhunter's Call* (Robert H. Perry); *The Headhunter Strategy* (Kenneth J. Cole); *The Directory of Executive Recruiters* (Kennedy Information); and *How to Get a Headhunter to Call* (Howard S. Freedman). An excellent book that reveals many of the job search secrets of headhunters, especially the critical interview, is Nick A. Corcodilos's *Ask the Headhunter* (Plume).

7. Marketing services

Marketing services represent an interesting combination of job search and executive search activities. They can cost $2,500 or more, and they work with individuals anticipating a starting salary of at least $75,000 but preferably over $100,000. These firms try to minimize the time and risk of applying for jobs. A typical operation begins with a client paying a $150 fee for developing psychological, skills, and interests profiles. Next, a marketing plan is outlined and a contract signed for specific services. The firm normally develops a slick "professional" resume and mails it along with a cover letter, to hundreds—maybe thousands—of firms. Clients are then briefed and sent to interview with interested employers. While you can save money and achieve the same results on your own, these firms do have one major advantage. They save you *time* by doing most of the work for you. Again, approach these services with caution. You can probably do just as well—if not better—on your own by following the step-by-step advice of this and other job search books.

8. **Women's centers and special career services**

Women's centers and special career services have been established to respond to the employment needs of special groups. Women's centers are particularly active in sponsoring career planning workshops and job information networks. These centers tend to be geared toward elementary job search activities, because their clientele largely consists of homemakers who are entering or re-entering the work force with little knowledge of the job market. Special career services arise for different categories of employees. For example, at various times unemployed aerospace engineers, teachers, veterans, air traffic controllers, and government employees, as well as older workers and retirees, have formed special groups for developing job search skills and sharing job leads.

9. **Testing and assessment centers**

Testing and assessment centers provide assistance for identifying vocational skills, interests, and objectives. Usually staffed by trained professionals, these centers administer several types of tests and charge from $300 to $1000 per person. You may wish to use some of these services if you feel our activities in Chapters 7, 8, and 9 generate insufficient information on your skills and interests to formulate your job objective. If you use such services, make sure you are given one or both of the two most popular and reliable tests: _Myers-Briggs Type Indicator_™ and the _Strong Interest Inventory._ You should find both tests helpful in better understanding your interests and decision-making styles. However, try our exercises before you hire a psychologist or visit a testing center. If you first complete these exercises, you will be in a better position to know exactly what you need from such centers. In many cases the career office at your local community college or women's center can administer these tests at minimum cost.

10. **Job fairs and career conferences**

Job fairs are organized by employment agencies, associations, consultants, headhunters, employment specialists, and many other groups. Career conferences are normally private affairs—by invitation only—organized by specific employers. Both are designed to link applicants to employers. Usually consisting of one- to two-day meetings in a hotel, employers meet with applicants as a group and on a one-to-one basis. Employers give presentations on their companies, applicants circulate resumes, and employers interview candidates. Many such conferences are organized to attract hard-to-recruit groups, such as IT specialists, engineers, computer programmers, and clerical and service workers. While private companies typically organize job fairs, federal, state, and local governments also use job fairs and career conferences to quickly recruit many specialized personnel. These fairs and conferences are excellent places to acquire job leads and information—if you get invited to the meetings or if they are open to the public. Employers pay for this service—not applicants.

11. **Professional associations**

Professional associations often provide placement assistance. This usually consists of listing job vacancies and organizing a job information exchange at annual conferences. Some associations operate online employment sites. Placement services available at annual conferences are good sources for making job contacts in different geographic locations within a particular professional field. But don't expect too much. Talking to people (networking) at professional conferences may yield better results than reading job listings and interviewing at conference placement centers.

Where to Look For Help

Finding a professional to assist you with your job search is relatively easy. You can start with the Yellow Pages of your telephone directory and take potluck. We highly recommend starting with your community college, library, state employment office, community women's center, or an appropriate professional association. Individuals in these organizations and institutions either provide free to inexpensive career services, or they can refer you to reputable individuals who provide such services. You also can consult various directories that list career professionals and employment services. Most libraries carry these four useful publications:

- *The Job Bank Guide to Employment Services, 2000-2001* (Holbrook, MA: Adams Media). Includes over 3,000 comprehensive profiles of employment agencies, executive search firms, temporary placement agencies, and resume/career counseling/testing services throughout the U.S. Enables individuals to pinpoint and assess various employment agencies and services within particular geographic areas.

- *Job Hunter's Sourcebook* (Detroit, MI: Gale Research), Michelle Le Compte (ed.). Lists sources of help-wanted ads, employer directories, employment agencies, placement services and other specific information sources for 155 specific careers.

- *What Color Is Your Parachute?* (Berkeley, CA: Ten Speed Press), Richard N. Bolles. The appendix of this annual guide includes the names, addresses, and telephone numbers of numerous career professionals deemed to be reliable by the author. Many have participated in the author's career training programs and thus share his job search and career planning approaches.

- *The World Almanac Job Finder's Guide 2001* (New York: St. Martin's Press), Les Krantz. This comprehensive job directory includes a section on "Services" which includes career counselors and vocational services, computer-search agencies, employment agencies, executive recruiters, sales recruiters, and temp agencies.

These books and directories also are available directly from Impact Publications (see order form or visit *www.impactpublications.com*).

Many career professionals also belong to a variety of professional associations. Five in particular are worth exploring:

- **National Board of Certified Counselors, Inc.:**   *www.nbcc.org*

- **National Career Development Association:**   *www.ncda.org*

- **Career Planning and Adult Development Network:**   *www.careernetwork.org*

- **Career Masters Institute:**   *www.cminstitute.com*

■ **Professional Resume Writing and
  Research Association (PRWRA):** *www.prwra.com*

Whatever you do, make sure you ask questions about the effectiveness of these professionals and their services. And, again, beware of anyone who wants to charge you up-front fees for promises of finding you a job. Testing, assessment service, and career counseling fees are legitimate professional charges. Promises to find you a job are not.

Choose the Best

Other types of career planning and employment services are growing and specializing in particular occupational fields. You may wish to use these services as a supplement to this book.

Whatever you do, proceed with caution, know exactly what you are getting into, and choose the best. Remember, there is no such thing as a free lunch, and you often get less than what you pay for. At the same time, the most expensive services are not necessarily the best. Indeed, the free and inexpensive career planning services offered by many community colleges—libraries, computerized career assessment programs, testing, and workshops—as well as the free Internet employment sites identified in Chapter 15 are often superior to fee-paid career services which can be expensive.

After reading this book, you should be able to make intelligent decisions about what, when, where, and with what results you can use professional assistance. Shop around, compare services and costs, ask questions, talk to former clients, and read the fine print with your lawyer before giving an employment expert a job using your hard-earned money.

6

Alternative Choices and the Right "Fit"

PPROACHES TO SELF-ASSESSMENT ARE NUMER-
ous and at times confusing. Everyone seems to offer their
own unique theory, approach, test, or exercise purporting to
provide insights into one's interests, values, skills, and
abilities. Many are psychological inventories designed to describe your
past and present orientation to work and other people. Other devices are
aimed at uncovering your past patterns of behavior that provide a basis
for predicting future behavior. All of these assessment devices are
supposed to give you a better understanding of who you are, assuming
you may be able to make better career and life choices with such
introspective information.

For the uninitiated, this can be a bewildering experience as they
attempt to acquire the most useful knowledge for directing their job
search. Which approach, for example, is best for you? Like a blind
person feeling the trunk of an elephant, they're not sure what they have
encountered. It could be an animal, but it might also be a tree.

Let's try to sort out the confusion and develop a clear idea of what
we are doing and where we are going by addressing some of the key
issues and questions involved in self-assessment. In so doing, you
should be in a better position to determine which approaches will be
most useful for your particular situation.

Alternative Approaches

You'll find numerous approaches to self-assessment. Some writers and career counselors claim you can do-it-on-your-own without the assistance of a professional. Indeed, some claim their self-directed exercises are just as valid as the testing instruments used by the professionals. Some claim they may even be superior to psychological testing. All you need to do is set aside a few hours of your time, complete the pencil-and-paper exercises, and analyze the information in reference to your particular job and career needs.

While we have no way of knowing how valid the self-directed approach is in comparison to many validated testing instruments, the self-directed approach does claim testimonials from thousands of people who claim it worked for them. When considering whether to use a self-directed versus a testing approach to self-assessment, your basic criteria for accepting an approach must be faith, common sense, and costs. In other words, is it worth your time and effort to engage in these exercises? If it sounds and feels good and others say it works, try it out; they won't hurt you. Self-directed approaches will only cost you time. If you spend the necessary time to complete the exercises, chances are you will gain a great deal of useful information on yourself for directing your job search. And you may join thousands of others with a testimonial that the exercises really worked for you.

> *Your basic criteria for accepting an approach must be faith, common sense, and costs.*

Most job and career books that include a self-assessment section use some variety of this self-directed approach. One of the most intensive and elaborate such exercises is Richard Bolles's *New Quick Job Hunting Map* (Ten Speed Press). We will have more to say later about this and other self-directed exercises.

But not all self-directed approaches are the same. Some are simple listings or checklists of information about your feelings, ideas, relationships, or decision-making style. For example, identify the 10 things you most like about your job. Or prioritize from a list of 100 work values the 10 that best describe what's important to you. Others are more elaborate self-graded tests such as our careering competencies exercise in Chapter 3. And still others are complicated and extremely time-consuming exercises that integrate facts and values into a system that analyzes several aspects of your job and career experiences. We'll share one of the most popular and useful such exercises with you in Chapter 9 when we integrate the simpler exercises of Chapters 7 and 8 into constructing a comprehensive picture of your major strengths.

Beware of Underlying Assumptions

You should also be aware that underlying every approach is an implicit theory or set of assumptions about how you behave. When related to issues about your future, each approach may generate certain advice on how you should relate to the world of work.

The major theory underlying the most popular self-directed exercises is a combination of **historical determinism** and **probability**: your future behavior will largely be a reflection of your past patterns of behavior. The emphasis here is on **patterns of behavior**. In the most sophisticated and sectarian form, these approaches direct you to identify your past patterns of motivated abilities and skills and then find jobs that will provide the best "fit" for your pattern. In the most extreme form, you will be told that you can't really do much about your patterns of behavior. They have been with you for years, and they will continue to dominate your behavior in the future. As this approach moves

> *Underlying every approach is an implicit theory, or set of assumptions, about how you behave.*

from description and explanation to prescription, it provides some sobering advice to those who believe in the power of self-transformation. Rather than try to change those patterns—which you probably can't or won't do anyway—it's best that you become more aware of them and learn to better live with yourself by seeking jobs and career opportunities that best use your "strengths."

Not a bad theory for most people who are generally pleased to learn that they indeed have these patterns of motivated abilities and skills. Many of them are elated to literally rediscover themselves after having completed exercises based on this theory. However, others are less enthusiastic after they learn the approaches largely generate information they already know about themselves.

Knowing your strengths is interesting descriptive and explanatory information about yourself, but it doesn't provide much prescriptive content for directing your future. For example, should you acquire new skills? What other jobs might be best suited for you? If you want to substantially increase your income, what should you do beyond what you have been doing in the past? Unfortunately, these self-directed exercises give you little guidance about your future since they are based upon historical information about you.

When proponents of this approach attempt to address questions about the future, they get themselves in a real quagmire by dispensing questionable how-to advice. The advice is usually the same and is part of the theory underlying the approach: *just follow your patterns.* This is very conservative and unenlightening advice that is sometimes further justified with reference to a conservative religious prescription—since God has established your pattern, you should learn to live with it and do the best you can within what are now your obvious limitations. There is little or no room in this approach for such notions as self-transformation—breaking out of one's past patterns to embark on a new future.

The clearest statements of this historical deterministic and probabilistic approach to self-assessment are found in *The Truth About You, What Color Is Your Parachute?*, and *Where Do I Go From Here With My Life?* The approach is also implicit in the structure of *The Quick Job Hunting Map.* It is also found in a host of other literature and self-directed exercises associated with the works of Haldane, Holland, Bolles, Crystal, and their followers. With certain qualifications and revisions, this approach also occupies a major place in this book.

> *Knowing your strengths is interesting information about you, but it doesn't provide much prescriptive content for directing your future.*

This is not to say these self-directed approaches do not work or are inherently deficient. Rather, they work well for thousands of people who embrace them and are willing to plan their futures around the notion of a pattern of motivated abilities and skills. Indeed, for 85 percent of the population, such an approach is very appropriate. They are not interested in self-transformation—just get a better handle on their strengths and direct their lives accordingly.

Our point is this: like any approach, these approaches have limitations. They can only take you so far, depending on what you want to do with your life. If you already know your strengths but want to acquire new strengths that will take you into new job and career directions, you'll simply have to use other approaches that are less historical and more future in orientation. The most important approaches will deal with issues of change and self-transformation.

A Job-Targeted Approach

Another problem with many self-assessment approaches is that they help you generate self-understanding about your past interests, values, abilities, and skills, but they don't go to the next important step—linking that self-knowledge to specific jobs and careers most appropriate for your particular mix of skills or pattern of motivated abilities and skills. Indeed many people already know what they do well and enjoy doing, but they want to know what alternative jobs and careers are the most likely candidates for their experience. Many teachers, for example, know they have strong organization, communication, and supervision skills, but they don't know what types of jobs outside teaching might offer better career opportunities, especially in terms of salaries and advancement. Many of the best jobs in the decade ahead outlined in Chapter 2, for example, may be appropriate for your particular mix of motivated skills and abilities.

> *For 85 percent of the population, the self-directed approach is very appropriate.*

Our approach to self-assessment incorporates many of the previous approaches and then targets the self-assessment information toward alternative jobs and careers. In other words, you first need to assess your strengths through self-assessment and then relate those strengths to specific jobs:

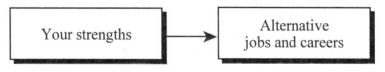

Once you know what jobs are likely to be the best "fit" for your particular mix of strengths, you will be well on the road to targeting your other job search activities (resumes, letters, networking, interviews) toward specific organizations, employers, and jobs.

Ask the Right Questions

We know that as much as 70 percent of the solution to most problems is found in first asking the right questions. In fact, you can easily reduce the complexity and confusion surrounding the many self-assessment approaches by focusing your attention on two basic questions:

1. What do you do well?

2. What do you enjoy doing?

The first question addresses your **skills and abilities**. The second question helps identify your **interests, values, motivations, and goals**. Once you've answered these questions, you next need to link your skills and abilities (Question 1) with your interests, values, and motivations (Question 2). When integrated with each other, these elements become your **motivated abilities and skills (MAS)**. When examined through a series of self-assessment exercises, they become identified as your **pattern** of motivated abilities and skills (MAS pattern). This pattern becomes your unique set of job and career **strengths** that are best used in particular types of jobs.

What you ultimately need to do is find the best "fit" between your strengths (MAS pattern) and alternative jobs. You do this by first learning what your strengths are (self-assessment centered on identifying your MAS pattern) and then aligning them with different jobs that seem conducive to your strengths.

Put another way, this process involves five distinct yet closely related steps in the process of discovering the best jobs for you. These steps are outlined on page 65. A sixth step would involve restating your general job and career objective (Step 4) at a more specific level for the jobs you seek. This objective would appear on your resume. It would also be the focus for your networking activities as well as a subject to be elaborated upon during job interviews.

The remaining chapters examine each of these steps in the process of discovering the right job for you. In addition, we return to the issue of historical determinism versus self-transformation in Chapter 10 when we examine alternative approaches to self-assessment.

FIND THE BEST JOBS PROCESS

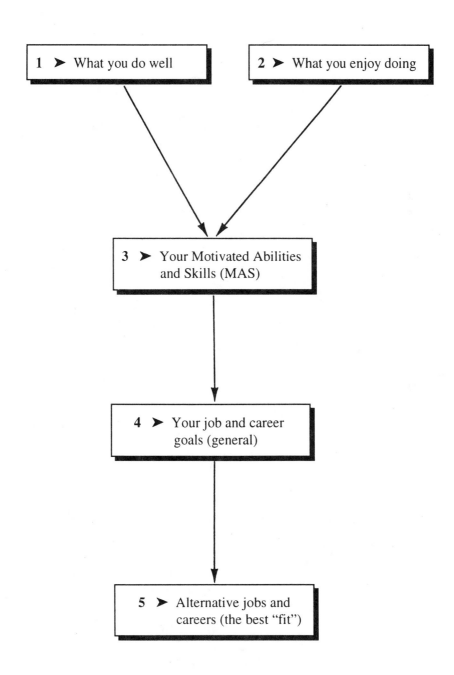

7

What You Do Well:
Your Skills and Abilities

W E LIVE IN A SKILLS-BASED SOCIETY WHERE IN-
dividuals market their skills to employers in exchange
for money, position, and power. The ease by which
individuals change jobs and careers is directly related to
their ability to communicate their skills to employers
and then transfer their skills to new work settings.

To best position yourself in the job markets of today and tomorrow,
you should pay particular attention to refining your present skills as well
as acquiring new and more marketable skills.

Know Your Skills

But before you can refine your skills or acquire additional skills, you
need to know what skills you presently possess. Unfortunately, few
people can identify and talk about their skills even though they possess
hundreds of skills which they use on a regular basis. This becomes a
real problem when they must communicate what they can do on a
resume or go to a job interview. Since employers want to know about
your specific abilities and skills, you must learn to both identify and
communicate your skills to employers. You should be able to explain
what it is you do well as well as give examples relevant to employers'
needs.

What skills do you already have to offer employers? If you have just completed an educational program, the skills you have to offer are most likely related to the subject matter you studied. If you are changing jobs or careers, the skills you wish to communicate to employers will be those things you already have demonstrated you can do in specific jobs.

Keep in mind that the skills required for *finding a job* are no substitute for the skills necessary for *doing the job*. Learning new skills requires a major investment of time, money, and effort. Nonetheless, the long-term pay-off should more than justify the initial costs. Indeed, research continues to show that well selected education and training provide the best returns on individual and societal investment.

Types of Skills

Most people possess two types of skills that define their accomplishments and strengths as well as enable them to enter and advance within the job market: work-content skills and functional skills. You need to acquaint yourself with these skills before communicating them to employers. These skills become the key language for communicating your qualifications to employers through your resumes and letters as well as in interviews.

We assume you have already acquired certain *work-content skills* necessary to function effectively in today's job market. These "hard skills" are easy to recognize since they are often identified as "qualifications" for specific jobs; they are the subject of most educational and training programs. Work-content skills tend to be technical and job-specific in nature. Examples of such skills include proficiency in designing websites, programming computers, teaching chemistry, or operating an X-ray machine. They may require formal training, are associated with specific trades or professions, and are used only in certain job and career settings. One uses a separate skills vocabulary, jargon, and subject matter for specifying technical qualifications of individuals entering and advancing in an occupation. While these skills do not transfer well from one occupation to another, they are critical for entering and advancing within certain occupations.

At the same time, you possess numerous *functional/transferable skills* employers readily seek along with your work-content skills. These "soft skills" are associated with numerous job settings, are mainly acquired through experience rather than formal training, and can be communicated through a general vocabulary. Functional/transferable skills are less easy to recognize since they tend to be linked to certain *personal characteristics* (energetic, intelligent, likable) and the ability to *deal with processes* (communicating, problem-solving, motivating) rather than *do things* (programming a computer, building a house, repairing air conditioners). While most people have only a few work-content skills, they may have numerous—as many as 300—functional/ transferable skills. These skills enable job seekers to more easily change jobs. But you must first be aware of your functional skills before you can relate them to the job market.

Most people view the world of work in traditional occupational job skill terms. This is a *structural view* of occupational realities. Occupational fields are seen as consisting of separate and distinct jobs which, in turn, require specific work-content skills. From this perspective, occupations and jobs are relatively self-contained entities. Social work, for example, is seen as being different from paralegal work; social workers, therefore, are not "qualified" to seek paralegal work.

> *Functional skills can be transferred from one job or career to another.*

On the other hand, a *functional view* of occupations and jobs emphasizes the similarity of job characteristics as well as common linkages between different occupations. Although the structure of occupations and jobs may differ, they have similar functions. They involve working with people, data, processes, and objects. If you work with people, data, processes, and objects in one occupation, you can transfer that experience to other occupations which have similar functions. Once you understand how your skills relate to the functions as well as investigate the structure of different occupations, you should be prepared to make job changes from one occupational field to another. Whether you possess the necessary work-content skills to qualify for entry into the other occupational field is another question altogether.

The skills we identify and help you organize in this chapter are the functional skills career counselors normally emphasize when advising clients to assess their *strengths*. In contrast to work-content skills, functional skills can be transferred from one job or career to another. They enable individuals to make some job and career changes without acquiring additional education and training. They constitute an important bridge for moving from one occupation to another.

Before you decide if you need more education or training, you should first assess both your functional and work-content skills to see how they can be transferred to other jobs and occupations. Once you do this, you should be better prepared to communicate your qualifications to employers with a rich skills-based vocabulary.

Your Strengths

Regardless of what combination of work-content and functional skills you possess, a job search must begin with identifying your strengths. Without knowing these, your job search will lack content and focus. After all, your goal should be to find a job that is fit for you rather than one you think you might be able to fit into. Of course, you also want to find a job for which there is a demand. This particular focus requires a well-defined approach to identifying and communicating your skills to others. You can best do this by asking the right questions about your strengths and then conducting a systematic self-assessment of what you do best.

Ask the Right Questions

Knowing the right questions to ask will save you time and steer you into productive job search channels from the very beginning. Asking the wrong questions can cripple your job search efforts and leave you frustrated. The questions must be understood from the perspectives of both employers and applicants.

Two of the most humbling questions you will encounter in your job search are *"Why should I hire you?"* and *"What are your weaknesses?"* While employers may not directly ask these questions, they are asking them nonetheless. If you can't answer these questions in a positive manner—directly, indirectly, verbally, or nonverbally—your job search will likely founder and you will join the ranks of the unsuccessful and disillusioned job searchers who feel something is wrong with them. Individuals who have lost their jobs are particularly vulnerable to these questions since many have lowered self-esteem and self-image as a result of the job loss. Many such people focus on what is wrong rather than what is right about themselves. Such thinking creates self-fulfilling prophecies and is self-destructive in the job market. By all means avoid such negative thinking.

Employers want to hire your *value* or *strengths*—not your weaknesses. Since it is easier to identify and interpret weaknesses, employers look for indicators of your strengths by trying to identify your weaknesses. The more successful you are in communicating your strengths to employers, the better off you will be in relation to both employers and fellow applicants.

Unfortunately, many people work against their own best interests. Not knowing their strengths, they market their weaknesses by first identifying job vacancies and then trying to fit their "qualifications" into job descriptions. This approach often frustrates applicants; it presents a picture of a job market that is not interested in the applicant's strengths. This leads some people toward acquiring new skills which they "hope" will be marketable, even though they do not enjoy using them. Millions of individuals find themselves in such misplaced situations. Your task is to avoid joining the ranks of the misplaced and unhappy work force by first understanding your skills and then relating them to your interests and goals. In so doing, you will be in a better position to target your efforts toward jobs that should become especially rewarding and fulfilling.

> *Your goal should be to find a job that is fit for you rather than one you think you might be able to fit into.*

Functional/Transferable Skills

We know most people stumble into jobs by accident. Some are at the right place at the right time to take advantage of opportunities. Others work hard at trying to fit into jobs listed in classified ads, employment agencies, and personnel offices; identified through friends and acquaintances; or found by knocking on doors. After 15 to 20 years in the work world, many people wish they had better planned their careers. All of a sudden they are unhappily locked into jobs because of retirement benefits, family responsibilities, and monthly mortgage payments.

After 10 or 20 years of work experience, most people have a good idea of what they don't like to do. While their values are more set than when they first began working, many people are still unclear as to what they do well and how their skills fit into the job market. What other jobs, for example, might they be qualified to perform? If they have the opportunity to change jobs or careers—either voluntarily or forced through termination—and find the time to plan the change, they can move into jobs and careers which fit their skills.

The key to understanding your non-technical strengths is to identify your transferable or functional skills. Once you have done this, you will be better prepared to identify what it is you want to do. Moreover, your self-image and self-esteem will improve. Better still, you will be prepared to communicate your strengths to others through a rich skills-based vocabulary. These outcomes are critically important for writing your resume and letters as well as for conducting informational and job interviews.

Let's illustrate the concept of functional/transferable skills for educators. Many educators view their skills in strict work-content terms—knowledge of a particular subject matter such as math, history, English, physics, or music. When looking for jobs outside education, many seek employment which will use their subject matter skills. But they soon discover non-educational institutions are not a ready market for such "skills."

On the other hand, educators possess many other skills that are directly transferable to business and industry.

> *Employers want to hire your value or strengths – not your weaknesses.*

Unaware of these skills, many educators fail to communicate their strengths to others. For example, research shows that graduate students in the humanities most frequently possess these transferable skills, in order of importance:

- critical thinking
- research techniques
- perseverance
- self-discipline
- insight
- writing

- general knowledge
- cultural perspective
- teaching ability
- self-confidence
- imagination
- leadership ability

Most functional/transferable skills can be classified into two general skills and trait categories—organizational/interpersonal skills and personality/work-style traits:

Organizational and Interpersonal Skills

- __ communicating
- __ problem solving
- __ analyzing/assessing

- __ troubleshooting
- __ implementing
- __ self-understanding

__ planning
__ decision-making
__ innovating
__ thinking logically
__ evaluating
__ identifying problems
__ synthesizing
__ forecasting
__ tolerating ambiguity
__ motivating
__ leading
__ selling
__ performing
__ reviewing
__ attaining
__ team building
__ updating
__ coaching
__ supervising
__ estimating
__ negotiating
__ administering

__ understanding
__ setting goals
__ conceptualizing
__ generalizing
__ managing time
__ creating
__ judging
__ controlling
__ organizing
__ persuading
__ encouraging
__ improving
__ designing
__ consulting
__ teaching
__ cultivating
__ advising
__ training
__ interpreting
__ achieving
__ reporting
__ managing

Personality and Work-Style Traits

__ diligent
__ patient
__ innovative
__ persistent
__ tactful
__ loyal
__ successful
__ versatile
__ enthusiastic
__ outgoing
__ expressive
__ adaptable
__ democratic
__ resourceful
__ determining

__ honest
__ reliable
__ perceptive
__ assertive
__ sensitive
__ astute
__ risk taker
__ easygoing
__ calm
__ flexible
__ competent
__ punctual
__ receptive
__ diplomatic
__ self-confident

__ creative   __ tenacious
__ open   __ discreet
__ objective   __ talented
__ warm   __ empathic
__ orderly   __ tidy
__ tolerant   __ candid
__ frank   __ adventuresome
__ cooperative   __ firm
__ dynamic   __ sincere
__ self-starter   __ initiator
__ precise   __ competent
__ sophisticated   __ diplomatic
__ effective   __ efficient

These are the types of traits you need to identify and then communicate to employers in your resumes and letters as well as during interviews.

Identify Your Skills

If you are just graduating from high school or college and do not know what you want to do, you probably should take a battery of vocational tests and psychological inventories to identify your interests and skills. These tests are listed in Chapter 8. If you don't fall into these categories of job seekers, chances are you don't need complex testing. You have experience, you have well-defined values, and you know what you don't like in a job. Therefore, we outline several alternative skills identification exercises—from simple to complex—for assisting you at this stage. We recommend using the most complete activity—the Motivated Skills Exercise—to gain a thorough understanding of your strengths.

Use the following exercises to identify both your work-content and transferable skills. These self-assessment techniques stress your positives or strengths rather than identify your negatives or weaknesses. As such, they should generate a rich vocabulary for communicating your "qualifications" to employers. Each exercise requires different investments of your time and effort as well as varying degrees of assistance from other people.

These exercises, however, should be used with caution. There is nothing magical nor particularly profound about them. Most are based upon a very simple and somewhat naive *deterministic theory of behavior*—your past patterns of behavior are good predictors of your future behavior. Not a bad theory for most individuals, but it is rather simplistic and disheartening for individuals who wish to, and can, break out of past patterns as they embark on a new future. Furthermore, most exercises are *historical devices.* They provide you with a clear picture of your past, which may or may not be particularly useful for charting your future. Nonetheless, these exercises do help individuals (1) organize data on themselves, (2) target their job search around clear objectives and skills, and (3) generate a rich vocabulary of skills and accomplishments for communicating strengths to potential employers.

If you feel these exercises are inadequate for your needs, by all means seek professional assistance from a testing or assessment center staffed by a licensed psychologist. These centers do in-depth testing which goes further than these self-directed skill exercises.

When using the following exercises, keep in mind that some individuals can and do change—often very dramatically—their behavior regardless of such deterministic and historical assessment devices. Much of the "motivation and success," "power of positive thinking," "thinking big," and "empowerment" literature, for example, challenges the validity of these standardized assessment tests that are used to predict or pattern future individual behavior. So be careful how you use such information for charting your career future. You *can* change your future. But at least get to know yourself before making the changes.

Checklist Method

This is the simplest method for identifying your strengths. Review the different transferable skills outlined on pages 72-73. Place a "1" in front of the skills that *strongly* characterize you; assign a "2" to those skills that describe you to a *large extent*; put a "3" before those that describe you to *some extent.* After completing this exercise, review the lists and rank order the 10 characteristics that best describe you on each list.

You'll also find other types of checklists on several websites of college and university career centers, such as the one operated by the University of California at Berkeley:

http://career.berkeley.edu/prep/prepskills.stm

Skills Map

Richard Bolles has produced two well-known exercises for identifying transferable skills based upon John Holland's typology of work environments. Both are historical devices structured around a deterministic theory of behavior. In his book, *The Three Boxes of Life* (Ten Speed Press), he develops a checklist of 100 transferable skills. They are organized into 12 categories or types of skills: using hands, body, words, senses, numbers, intuition, analytical thinking, creativity, helpfulness, artistic abilities, leadership, and follow-through.

Bolles's second exercise, *The Quick Job Hunting Map*, expands upon this first one. The *Map* is a checklist of 222 skills. This exercise requires you to identify seven of your most satisfying accomplishments, achievements, jobs, or roles. After writing a page about each experience, you relate each to the checklist of 222 skills. The *Map* should give you a comprehensive picture of what skills you (1) use most frequently, and (2) enjoy using in satisfying and successful settings. While this exercise may take six hours to complete, it yields an enormous amount of data on past strengths. Furthermore, the *Map* generates a rich skills vocabulary for communicating your strengths to others. The *Map* is found in the resource section of Bolles's *What Color Is Your Parachute?* (Ten Speed Press) or it can be purchased separately in beginning, advanced, or new versions from Ten Speed Press. His books, as well as the latest version of his popular *New Quick Job Hunting Map*, can be ordered directly from Impact Publications by completing the order form at the end of this book.

Autobiography of Accomplishments

Write a lengthy essay about your life accomplishments. This could range from 20 to 100 pages. After completing the essay, go through it page by page to identify what you most enjoyed doing (working with different kinds of information, people, and things) and what skills you used most frequently as well as enjoyed using. Finally, identify those skills you wish to continue using. After analyzing and synthesizing this data, you should have a relatively clear picture of your strongest skills.

Computerized Assessment Systems

While the previous self-directed exercises required you to either respond to checklists of skills or reconstruct and analyze your past job experiences, several computerized self-assessment programs are designed to help individuals identify their skills. Many of the programs are available in schools, colleges, and libraries; some can be ordered directly from Impact Publications (see order form at the end of this book or visit their online resource center: *www.impactpublications.com*). Some of the most widely used programs include:

- *Choices*
- *Cambridge Career Counseling System*
- *Career Information System* (CIS)
- *Career Navigator*
- *Discover*
- *Guidance Information System* (GIS)
- *Job Browser Pro*
- *Jumpstart Your Job Skills*™
- *SIGI-Plus* (System of Interactive Gudance and Information)
- *SkillsUp*™

Most of these comprehensive career planning programs do much more than just assess skills. As we will see in Chapter 9, they also integrate other key components in the career planning process— interests, goals, related jobs, college majors, education and training programs, and job search plans. These programs are widely available in schools, colleges, and libraries across the country. If you are uncertain where to find them, you might first check with the career or counseling center at your local community college to see what computerized career assessment systems are available for your use. Relatively easy to use, they generate a great deal of useful career planning information. Many will print out a useful analysis of how your interests and skills are related to specific jobs and careers. Some, such as *Job Browser Pro*, can be expanded to include a nearly 100-page detailed report on interests, skills, abilities, and specific jobs related to an individual's assessment profile.

Online Exercises, Tests, and Inventories

Many assessment instruments also are available on the World Wide Web. They come in many forms, from pencil-and-paper exercises to computerized self-scoring tests and counselor-assisted (via telephone) inventories. A disproportionate number of these devices are psychological tests and inventories based upon the *Myers-Briggs Type Indicator* or the *Self-Directed Search*. We review the major assessment websites, such as *www.careerhub.org* and *www.careerlab.com*, in Chapter 15.

8

What You Enjoy Doing:
Your Interests and Values

KNOWING WHAT YOU DO WELL IS ESSENTIAL FOR understanding your strengths and for linking your capabilities to specific jobs. However, just knowing your abilities and skills will not give your job search the direction it needs for finding the right job. You also need to know your work values, interests, and preferences. These are the basic building blocks for setting goals and targeting your abilities toward specific jobs.

Take, for example, the individual who can word process 120 words a minute. While this person possesses a highly marketable skill, if the person doesn't enjoy using this skill and is more interested in working outdoors, this will not become a *motivated skill*; the individual will most likely not pursue a word processing job. Your interests and values will determine whether or not certain skills should play a central role in your job search.

Interests and the *"Aha"* Effect

We all have interests. Most change over time. Many of your interests may center on your present job whereas others relate to activities that define your hobbies and leisure activities. A good place to start identifying your interests is by examining the information and exercises

77

found in both *The Guide For Occupational Exploration* and *The Enhanced Guide to Occupational Exploration*. Widely used by students and others first entering the job market, these guides also are relevant to individuals who already have work experience. They classify all jobs in the U.S. into 12 interest areas. Examine the following list of interest areas. In the first column check those work areas that appeal to you. In the second column rank order those areas you checked in the first column. Start with "1" to indicate the most interesting:

Your Work Interests

Yes/No (x)	Ranking (1-12)	Interest Area
___	___	**Artistic:** An interest in creative expression of feelings or ideas.
___	___	**Scientific:** An interest in discovering, collecting, and analyzing information about the natural world, and in applying scientific research findings to problems in medicine, the life sciences, and the nature sciences.
___	___	**Plants and animals:** An interest in working with plants and animals, usually outdoors.
___	___	**Protective:** An interest in using authority to protect people and property.
___	___	**Mechanical:** An interest in applying mechanical principles to practical situations by using machines or hand tools.
___	___	**Industrial:** An interest in repetitive, concrete, organized activities done in a factory setting.
___	___	**Business detail:** An interest in organized, clearly defined activities requiring accuracy and attention to details (office settings).

___   ___   **Selling:** An interest in bringing others to a particular point of view by personal persuasion, using sales and promotion techniques.

___   ___   **Accommodating:** An interest in catering to the wishes and needs of others, usually on a one-to-one basis.

___   ___   **Humanitarian:** An interest in helping others with their mental, spiritual, social, physical, or vocational needs.

___   ___   **Leading and influencing:** An interest in leading and influencing others by using high-level verbal or numerical abilities.

___   ___   **Physical performing:** An interest in physical activities performed before an audience.

The Guide For Occupational Exploration also includes other checklists relating to home-based and leisure activities that may or may not relate to your work interests. If you are unclear about your work interests, you might want to consult these other interest exercises. You may discover that some of your home-based and leisure activity interests should become your work interests. Examples of such interests include:

Leisure and Home-Based Interests

___ Acting in a play or amateur variety show.

___ Advising family members on their personal problems.

___ Announcing or emceeing a program.

___ Applying first aid in emergencies as a volunteer.

___ Building model airplanes, automobiles, or boats.

___ Building or repairing radio or television sets.

___ Buying large quantities of food or other products for an organization.

___ Campaigning for political candidates or issues.

___ Canning and preserving food.

___ Carving small wooden objects.

___ Coaching children or youth in sports activities.

___ Collecting experiments involving plants.

___ Conducting house-to-house or telephone surveys for a PTA or other organization.

___ Creating or styling hairdos for friends.

___ Designing your own greeting cards and writing original verses.

___ Developing film.

___ Doing impersonations.

___ Doing public speaking or debating.

___ Entertaining at parties or other events.

___ Helping conduct physical exercises for disabled people.

___ Making ceramic objects.

___ Modeling clothes for a fashion show.

___ Mounting and framing pictures.

___ Nursing sick pets.

___ Painting the interior or exterior of a home.

___ Playing a musical instrument.

___ Refinishing or re-upholstering furniture.

___ Repairing electrical household appliances.

___ Repairing the family car.

___ Repairing or assembling bicycles.

___ Repairing plumbing in the house.

___ Speaking on radio or television.

___ Taking photographs.

___ Teaching in Sunday School.

___ Tutoring pupils in school subjects.

___ Weaving rugs or making quilts.

___ Writing articles, stories, or plays.

___ Writing songs for club socials or amateur plays.

Indeed, many people turn hobbies or home activities into full-time jobs after deciding that such "work" is what they really enjoy doing.

Other popular exercises designed to identify your work interests include John Holland's *The Self-Directed Search*, which is found in his book, *Making Vocational Choices: A Theory of Careers*. It is also published as a separate testing instrument, *The Self-Directed Search– A Guide to Educational and Vocational Planning*. Developed from Holland's Vocational Preference Inventory, this popular self-adminis- tered, self-scored, and self-interpreted inventory helps individuals quickly identify what type of work environment they seek—realistic, investigative, artistic, social, enterprising, or conventional—and aligns these work environments with lists of common occupational titles. An easy exercise to use, it gives you a quick overview of your orientation toward different types of work settings that interest you.

Holland's self-directed search is also the basic framework used in developing Bolles's *The Quick Job Hunting Map* as found in his *What Color Is Your Parachute?*, *The New Quick Job Hunting Map*, *Three Boxes of Life*, and *Where Do I Go From Here With My Life?* books.

For more sophisticated treatments of work interests, which are also validated through testing procedures, contact a career counselor, women's center, or testing and assessment center for information on these tests:

- *Myers-Briggs Type Indicator®*
- *Strong Interest Inventory*
- *Edwards Personal Preference Schedule*
- *Kuder Occupational Interest Survey*
- *APTICOM*
- *Jackson Vocational Interest Survey*
- *Ramak Inventory*
- *Vocational Interest Inventory*
- *Career Assessment Inventory*
- *Temperament and Values Inventory*

Numerous other job and career interest inventories are also available. For further information, contact a career counselor or consult Educational Testing Service which compiles such tests. *The ETS Test Collection Catalog* (New York: Oryx Press), which is available in many library reference sections, lists most of these tests. The *Mental Measurements Yearbook* (Lincoln, NE: University of Nebraska Press) also surveys many of the major testing and assessment instruments.

You'll also find numerous online career tests and inventories. We outline several such resources in Chapter 15.

Keep in mind that not all testing and assessment instruments used by career counselors are equally valid for career planning purposes, nor are they particularly useful for individual decision-making. Many appear to be a scientific form of "snake oil" embellished with test questions, scoring devices, typologies, and statistics. Most are designed to help you **better understand yourself**, which means they can be used in a variety of counseling situations, from dealing with marital problems, child abuse, and alcoholism to helping make career decisions. Most also are developed around typologies that may give you little useful information beyond the *"aha"* effect—a momentary confirmation that indeed the typology you fit into appears to describe the "unique you." As with most typological analyses, they are "more or less" useful —but never definitive.

> *Many of these assessment devices appear to be a scientific form of "snake oil" embellished with test questions, scoring devices, typologies, and statistics.*

While the Strong Interest Inventory appears to be the most relevant for career decision-making, the Myers-Briggs Type Indicator® personality inventory has become extremely popular during the past 15 years. Based on Carl Gustav Jung's personality preference theory—which was derived and further extended from a simplistic 19th century European academic tradition of understanding phenomena through analytical constructs or typologies—the Myers-Briggs Type Indicator®, or MBTI personality inventory, is used extensively by psychologists and career counselors for identifying personality types and preferences. However, the MBTI is more useful for measuring individual personality and decision-making styles than for predicting career choices. It is most widely used in pastoral counseling, student personnel, and business and religious organizations for measuring personality and decision-making styles. For more information on the MBTI, see Isabel Briggs Myers's *Introduction to Type: A Description of the Theory and Applications of the Myers-Briggs Type Indicator* (Consulting Psychologists Press) and *Gifts Differing* (Davies-Black).

Many career counselors find Holland's *The Self-Directed Search* an excellent self-directed alternative to these professionally administered and interpreted tests. While not as sophisticated nor as well developed as some of the standard scored testing devices, nonetheless, this is another simplistic typological approach that is "more or less" useful. This self-assessment instrument is found in John J. Holland, *Making Vocational Choices: A Theory of Careers* (Prentice-Hall) and *The Psychology of Vocational Choices*, and *The Dictionary of Holland Occupational Codes* (Consulting Psychologists Press).

For self-assessment devices that synthesize the Myers-Briggs Type Indicator®, Holland vocational choices, and other popular instruments, see Gerald M. Sturman, *The Career Discovery Project* (Doubleday). His synthesis of several self-assessment instruments involving job satisfaction, motivation, career type, skills, internal barriers, and values and professional development needs results in a comprehensive *"Personal Career Profile®"* that should help individuals in writing resumes and preparing for the job interview.

Work Values

Work values are those things you like to do. They give you pleasure and enjoyment. Most jobs involve a combination of likes and dislikes. By identifying what you both like and dislike about jobs, you should be able to better identify jobs that involve tasks that you will most enjoy.

Several exercises can help you identify your work values. First, identify what most satisfies you about work by completing this exercise:

My Work Values

I prefer employment which enables me to:

____ contribute to society	____ be creative
____ have contact with people	____ supervise others

___ work alone	___ work with details
___ work with a team	___ gain recognition
___ compete with others	___ acquire security
___ make decisions	___ make money
___ work under pressure	___ help others
___ use power and authority	___ solve problems
___ acquire new knowledge	___ take risks
___ be a recognized expert	___ work at own pace

Select four work values from the above list which are the most important to you and list them in the space below. List any other work values (desired satisfactions) which were not listed above but are nonetheless important to you:

1. _____

2. _____

3. _____

4. _____

_____

_____

Another approach to identifying work values is outlined in *The Guide For Occupational Exploration*. If you feel you need to go beyond the above exercises, try this one. In the first column check those values that are most important to you. In the second column rank order the five most important values:

Ranking Work Values

Yes/No (x)	Ranking (1-5)	Work Values
____	____	**Adventure:** Working in a job that requires taking risks.
____	____	**Authority:** Working in a job in which you use your position to control others.
____	____	**Competition:** Working in a job in which you compete with others.
____	____	**Creativity and self-expression:** Working in a job in which you use your imagination to find new ways to do or say something.
____	____	**Flexible work schedule:** Working in a job in which you choose your hours to work.
____	____	**Helping others:** Working in a job in which you provide direct services to persons with problems.
____	____	**High salary:** Working in a job where many workers earn a large amount of money.
____	____	**Independence:** Working in a job in which you decide for yourself what work to do and how to do it.
____	____	**Influencing others:** Working in a job in which you influence the opinions of others or decisions of others.
____	____	**Intellectual stimulation:** Working in a job which requires a great amount of thought and reasoning.

___ ___ **Leadership:** Working in a job in which you direct, manage, or supervise the activities of others.

___ ___ **Outside work:** Working outdoors.

___ ___ **Persuading:** Working in a job in which you personally convince others to take certain actions.

___ ___ **Physical work:** Working in a job which requires substantial physical activity.

___ ___ **Prestige:** Working in a job which gives you status and respect in the community.

___ ___ **Public attention:** Working in a job in which you attract immediate notice because of appearance or activity.

___ ___ **Public contact:** Working in a job in which you deal with the public daily.

___ ___ **Recognition:** Working in a job in which you gain public notice.

___ ___ **Research work:** Working in a job in which you search for and discover new facts and develop ways to apply them.

___ ___ **Routine work:** Working in a job in which you follow established procedures requiring little change.

___ ___ **Seasonal work:** Working in a job in which you are employed only at certain times of the year.

___ ___ **Travel:** Working in a job in which you take frequent trips.

—— —— **Variety:** Working in a job in which your duties change frequently.

—— —— **Work with children:** Working in a job in which you teach or care for children.

—— —— **Work with hands:** Working in a job in which you use your hands or hand tools.

—— —— **Work with machines or equipment:** Working in a job in which you use machines or equipment.

—— —— **Work with numbers:** Working in a job in which you use mathematics or statistics.

Second, develop a comprehensive list of your past and present *job frustrations and dissatisfactions*. This should help you identify negative factors you should avoid in future jobs.

My Job Frustrations and Dissatisfactions

List as well as rank order as many past and present things that frustrate or make you dissatisfied and unhappy in job situations:

Rank

1. _____ ____

2. _____ ____

3. _____ ____

4. _____ ____

5. _____ ____

6. _____ ____

7. _____ ____

8. _____ ____

9. _____ ____

10. _____ ____

11. _____ ____

12. _____ ____

Third, brainstorm a list of "Ten or More Things I Love to Do." Identify which ones could be incorporated into what kinds of work environments:

Ten or More Things I Love To Do

Item	Related Work Environment
1. _____	_____
2. _____	_____
3. _____	_____
4. _____	_____
5. _____	_____
6. _____	_____
7. _____	_____
8. _____	_____
9. _____	_____
10. _____	_____

Fourth, list at least ten things you most enjoy about work and rank each item accordingly:

Ten Things I Enjoy the Most About Work

                                                        Rank

1. _____   _____

2. _____   _____

3. _____   _____

4. _____   _____

5. _____   _____

6. _____   _____

7. _____   _____

8. _____   _____

9. _____   _____

10. _____   _____

Fifth, you should also identify the types of interpersonal environments you prefer working in. Do this by specifying the types of people you like and dislike associating with:

Interpersonal Environments

Characteristics of people I like working with:	Characteristics of people I dislike working with:
_____	_____
_____	_____
_____	_____
_____	_____
_____	_____

_____   _____

_____   _____

_____   _____

_____   _____

_____   _____

_____   _____

Computerized Assessment Systems

Several computerized self-assessment programs identified in Chapter 7 (page 76) largely focus on career interests and values. Again, you may be able to get access to these and other relevant computerized assessment programs through your local community college, career center, or library.

Your Future As Objectives

All of these exercises are designed to explore your past and present work-related values. At the same time, you need to project your values into the *future*. What, for example, do you want to do over the next 10 to 20 years? We'll return to this type of value question when we address in Chapter 11 the critical objective-setting stage of the job search process.

9

Identify Your Motivated Abilities and Skills (MAS)

ONCE YOU KNOW WHAT YOU DO WELL AND ENJOY doing, you next need to analyze those interests, values, abilities, and skills that form a **recurring motivated pattern**. This "pattern" is the single most important piece of information you need to know about yourself in the whole self-assessment process. Knowing your skills and abilities alone without knowing how they relate to your interests and values will not give you the necessary direction for finding the best jobs for you. You simply *must* know your pattern *before* you focus on particular jobs.

What's Your MAS?

The concept of motivated abilities and skills (MAS) enables us to relate your interests and values to your skills and abilities. But how do we identify your MAS beyond the questions/exercises outlined thus far?

Your pattern of motivated abilities and skills becomes evident once you analyze your *achievements* or *accomplishments*. For it is your achievements that tell us what you both did well and enjoyed doing. If we analyze and synthesize your key achievements, we are likely to identify a *recurring pattern* that most likely goes back to your child-hood and which will continue to characterize your future achievements.

An equally useful exercise would be to identify your weaknesses by analyzing your failures. These, too, would fall into recurring patterns. Understanding what your weaknesses are might help you avoid jobs and work situations that bring out the worst in you. Indeed, you may learn more about yourself by analyzing your failures than by focusing solely on your accomplishments.

For now, let's focus on your positives rather than identify your negatives. After you complete the strength exercises in this chapter, you may want to reverse the procedures to identify your weaknesses.

Numerous self-directed exercises can assist you in identifying your pattern of motivated abilities and skills. The basic requirements for making these exercises work for you are time and analytical ability. You must spend a great deal of time detailing your achievements by looking at your history of accomplishments. Once you complete the historical reconstruction task, you must comb through your "stories" to identify recurring themes and patterns. This requires a high level of analytical ability which you may or may not possess. If analysis and synthesis are not two of your strong skills, you may want to seek assistance from a friend or professional who is good at analyzing and synthesizing information presented in narrative form. Career management firms such as Bernard Haldane Associates (*www.jobhunting.com*) and People Management, Inc. (*www.jobfit-pmi.com*) use of this type of motivated pattern approach; they should be able to assist you.

Several paper and pencil exercises are designed to help identify your pattern of motivated abilities and skills. We outline some of the most popular and thorough such exercises that have proved useful to thousands of people.

The Skills Map

Richard Bolles's *Quick Job Hunting Map* has become a standard self-assessment tool for thousands of job seekers and career changers who are willing to spend the time and effort necessary for discovering their pattern of motivated abilities and skills. Offering a checklist of over 200 skills organized around John Holland's concept of *The Self-Directed Search* for defining work environments (realistic, investigative, artistic, social, enterprising, and conventional), the *Map* requires you to identify seven of your most satisfying accomplishments, achievements, jobs, or roles. After detailing each achievement, you analyze the details of each in relation to the checklist of skills. Once you do this for all seven achievements, you should have a comprehensive picture of what skills you (1) use most frequently, and (2) enjoy using in satisfying and successful settings. This exercise not only yields an enormous amount of information on your interests, values, skills, and abilities, it also assists you in the process of analyzing the data. If done properly, the *Map* should also generate a rich "skills" vocabulary which you should use in your resumes and letters as well as in interviews.

The *Map* is available in different forms and for different levels of experience. The most popular versions are found in the resource section of Bolles's *What Color Is Your Parachute?* and *The Three Boxes of Life* as well as in a separate publication entitled *The New Quick Job Hunting Map*. These three publications can be ordered directly from Impact Publications by completing the order information at the end of this book. The *Map* is also available in other versions, from beginning to advanced, which are most conveniently available directly from the publisher, Ten Speed Press (P.O. Box 7123, Berkeley, CA 94707).

We highly recommend using the Map because of the ease in which it can be used. If you will spend the six to 20 hours necessary to complete it properly, the *Map* will give you some important information about yourself. Unfortunately, many people become overwhelmed by the exercise and either decide not to complete it, or they try to save time by not doing it according to the directions. You simply must follow the directions and spend the time and effort necessary if you want to get the maximum benefit from this exercise.

> *Once you uncover your pattern, get prepared to acknowledge it and live with it in the future.*

Keep in mind that like most self-assessment devices based on simplistic analytical constructs, typologies, or classification systems (*"you belong in this cell"*), there is nothing magical about the *Map*. Like many other testing devices, it often results in the *"aha"* effect but gives users little decision-making power. Its basic organizing principles are simple. Like other exercises designed to uncover your pattern of motivated abilities and skills, this one is based on a theory of historical determinism and probability. In other words, once you discover your MAS pattern, get prepared to become "realistic" about yourself—acknowledge it and live with it in the future!

Autobiography of Accomplishments

Less structured than the *Map* device, this exercise requires you to write a lengthy essay about your life accomplishments. Your essay may run anywhere from 20 to 200 pages. After completing it, go through it page by page to identify what you most enjoyed doing (working with different kinds of data, people, processes, objects) and what skills you used most frequently as well as enjoyed using. Finally, identify those skills you wish to continue using. After analyzing and synthesizing this data, you should have a relatively clear picture of your strongest skills.

This exercise requires a great deal of self-discipline and analytic skill. To do it properly, you must write as much as possible, and in as much detail as possible, about your accomplishments. The richer the detail, the better will be your analysis.

Motivated Skills Exercise

Our final exercise is one of the most complex and time-consuming self-assessment exercises. However, it yields some of the best data on motivated abilities and skills, and it is especially useful for those who feel they need a more thorough analysis of their past achievements. This device is widely used by career counselors. Initially developed by Bernard Haldane Associates, this particular exercise is variously referred to as *"Success Factor Analysis," "System to Identify Motivated Skills,"* or *"Intensive Skills Identification."*

This technique helps you identify which skills you *enjoy* using. While you can use this technique on your own, it is best to work with someone else. Since you will need six to eight hours to properly complete this exercise, divide your time into two or three work sessions.

The exercise consists of six steps. The steps follow the basic pattern of generating raw data, identifying patterns, analyzing the data through reduction techniques, and synthesizing the patterns into a transferable skills vocabulary. You need strong analytical skills to complete this exercise on your own. The six steps include:

1. **Identify 15-20 achievements:** These consist of things you enjoyed doing, believe you did well, and felt a sense of satisfaction, pride, or accomplishment in doing. You can see yourself performing at your best and enjoying your experiences

when you analyze your achievements. This information reveals your motivations since it deals entirely with your voluntary behavior. In addition, it identifies what is right with you by focusing on your positives and strengths. Identify achievements throughout your life, beginning with your childhood. Your achievements should relate to specific experiences—not general ones—and may be drawn from work, leisure, education, military, or home life. Put each achievement at the top of a separate sheet of paper. For example, your achievements might appear as follows:

Sample Achievement Statements

"When I was 10 years old, I started a small paper route and built it up to the largest in my district."

"I started playing chess in ninth grade and earned the right to play first board on my high school chess team in my junior year."

"Learned to play the piano and often played for church services while in high school."

"Designed and constructed a dress for a 4-H demonstration project."

"Although I was small compared to other guys, I made the first string on my high school football team."

"I graduated from high school with honors even though I was very active in school clubs and had to work part-time."

"I was the first in my family to go to college and one of the few from my high school. Worked part-time and summers. A real struggle, but I made it."

"Earned an 'A' grade on my senior psychology project from a real tough professor."

_____

"Finished my master's degree while working full-time and attending to my family responsibilities."

_____

"Proposed a chef's course for junior high boys. Got it approved. Developed it into a very popular elective."

_____

"Designed the plans for our house and had it constructed within budget." _____

2. Prioritize your seven most significant achievements.

Your Most Significant Achievements

1. _____

2. _____

3. _____

4. _____

5. _____

6. _____

7. _____

3. Write a full page on each of your prioritized achievements. You should describe:

- How you initially became involved.
- The details of *what you did* and *how you did it.*
- What was especially enjoyable or satisfying to you.

Use copies of the "Detailing Your Achievements" form on page 97 to outline your achievements.

Detailing Your Achievements

ACHIEVEMENT # ___: _____

_____

_____

1. How did I initially become involved? _____

_____

_____

_____

2. What did I do? _____

_____

_____

_____

_____

3. How did I do it? _____

_____

_____

_____

_____

4. What was especially enjoyable about doing it?

_____

_____

_____

_____

4. **Elaborate on your achievements:** Have one or two other people interview you. For each achievement have them note on a separate sheet of paper any terms used to reveal your skills, abilities, and personal qualities. To elaborate details, the interviewer(s) may ask:

   - What was involved in the achievement?
   - What was your part?
   - What did you actually do?
   - How did you go about that?

   Clarify any vague areas by providing an example or illustration of what you actually did. Probe with the following questions:

   - Would you elaborate on one example of what you mean?
   - Could you give me an illustration?
   - What were you good at doing?

   This interview should clarify the details of your activities by asking only "what" and "how" questions. It should take 45 to 90 minutes to complete. Make copies of the "Strength Identification Interview" form on page 99 to guide you through this interview.

5. **Identify patterns by examining the interviewer's notes:** Together identify the recurring skills, abilities, and personal qualities *demonstrated* in your achievements. Search for patterns. Your skills pattern should be clear at this point; you should feel comfortable with it. If you have questions, review the data. If you disagree with a conclusion, disregard it. The results must accurately and honestly reflect how you operate.

6. **Synthesize the information by clustering similar skills into categories:** For example, your skills might be grouped in the following manner (top of page 100):

Strength Identification Interview

Interviewee _____   Interviewer _____

INSTRUCTIONS: For each achievement experience, identify the **skills and abilities** the achiever actually demonstrated. Obtain details of the experience by asking *what* was involved with the achievement and *how* the individual made the achievement happen. Avoid "why" questions, which tend to mislead. Ask for examples or illustrations of what and how.

Achievement #1:

Achievement #2:

Achievement #3:

Recurring abilities and skills:

Synthesized Skill Clusters

Investigate/Survey/Read Inquire/Probe/Question	Teach/Train/Drill Perform/Show/Demonstrate
Learn/Memorize/Practice Evaluate/Appraise/Assess Compare	Construct/Assemble/Put together
	Organize/Structure/Provide definition/Plan/Chart course Strategize/Coordinate
Influence/Involve/Get participation/Publicize Promote	
	Create/Design/Adapt/Modify

This exercise yields a relatively comprehensive inventory of your skills. The information will better enable you to use a *skills vocabulary* when identifying your objective, writing your resume and letters, and interviewing. Your self-confidence and self-esteem should increase accordingly.

Other Alternatives

Several other techniques also can help you identify your motivated abilities and skills:

1. List all of your hobbies and analyze what you do in each, which ones you like the most, what skills you use, and your accomplishments.

2. Conduct a job analysis by writing about your past jobs and identifying which skills you used in each job. Cluster the skills into related categories and prioritize them according to your preferences.

3. Purchase a copy of Arthur F. Miller and Ralph T. Mattson's *The Truth About You* and work through the exercises found in the Appendix. While its overt religious message, extreme deterministic approach, and laborious exercises may turn you off, it's a useful book nonetheless. This is an abbreviated version of the authors' SIMA (System for Identifying Motivated Abilities) technique used by their career counseling firm, People Management, Inc. (*www.jobfit-pmi.com*).

4. Get a copy of Nella Barkley and Eric Sandburg's *The Crystal-Barkley Guide to Taking Charge of Your Career* (Workman) and complete its various chapters. This book is based on the pioneering self-assessment work of John Crystal.

5. Complete John Holland's *The Self-Directed Search.* It's in his book, *Making Vocational Choices: A Theory of Careers*, or in a separate publication entitled *The Self-Directed Search: A Guide to Educational and Vocational Planning.*

Benefit From Redundancy

The self-directed MAS exercises generate similar information. They identify interests, values, abilities, and skills you already possess. While aptitude and achievement tests may yield similar information, the self-directed exercises have three major advantages over standardized tests: less expensive, self-monitored, and measure motivation *and* ability. Hopefully, they will take you beyond the *"aha"* effect associated with many standardized tests and online inventories (see Chapter 15).

Completing each exercise demands a different investment of your time. Writing your life history and completing the Motivated Skills Exercise as well as Bolles's *Map* are the most time consuming. On the other hand, Holland's *Self-Directed Search* can be completed in a few minutes. But the more time you invest with each technique, the more useful information you will generate.

We recommend creating redundancy by using at least two or three different techniques. This will help reinforce and confirm the validity of your observations and interpretations. If you have a great deal of work experience, we recommend using the more thorough exercises. The more you put into these techniques and exercises, the greater the benefit to other stages of your job search. You will be well prepared to target your job search toward specific jobs that fit your MAS as well as communicate your qualifications loud and clear to employers. A carefully planned career or career change should not do less than this.

Bridging Your Past and Future

Many people want to know about their future. If you expect the self-assessment techniques in Chapters 7, 8, and 9 to spell out your future, you will be disappointed. Fortune tellers, horoscopes, and various forms of mysticism and "positive thinking" may be what you need.

These are historical devices which integrate past achievements, abilities, and motivations into a coherent framework for projecting future performance. They clarify past strengths and recurring motivations for targeting future jobs. Abilities and motivations are the *qualifications* employers expect for particular jobs. Qualifications consist of your past experience *and* your motivated abilities and skills.

The assessment techniques provide a bridge between your past and future. As such, they treat your future preferences and performance as functions of your past experiences and demonstrated abilities. This common sense notion is shared among employers: past performance is the best predictor of future performance.

> **Past performance is the best predictor of future performance.**

Yet, employers want to hire a person's *future* rather than their past. And herein lies an important problem you can help employers overcome. Getting the job that is right for you entails communicating to prospective employers that you have the necessary qualifications. Indeed, employers will look for signs of your future productivity *for them*. You are an unknown and risky quantity. Therefore, you must communicate evidence of your past productivity. This evidence is revealed clearly in your past achievements as outlined in our assessment techniques. In the end, these assessment devices generate a rich vocabulary for communicating skills, abilities, interests, and accomplishments in the language of employers.

The overall value of using these assessment techniques is that they should enhance your occupational mobility over the long run. The major thrust of all these techniques is to identify abilities and skills which are *transferable* to different work environments. This is particularly important if you are making a career change. You must overcome employers' negative expectations and objections by clearly communicating your transferable abilities and skills in the most positive terms possible. These assessment techniques are designed to do precisely that.

10

Beyond Self-Knowledge to Self-Transformation

NOT EVERYONE DESIRES TO SEE THEIR FUTURE become a replay of their past. Many have dreams, some of which seem to be impossible dreams. Indeed, many people aspire to achieve goals that may initially appear to be beyond their immediate capacity. Setting ostensibly *unrealistic goals*, through a combination of talent, dogged persistence, and luck, many of these people eventually do achieve their dreams.

Why Limit Yourself?

While most people may be content in identifying their motivated abilities and skills and pursuing jobs and careers that best fit their MAS patterns, other people desire to break out of past patterns as they embark on a new and uncharted future. For this latter group, identifying one's past patterns of motivated abilities and skills may be interesting self-knowledge, but it does not help put them on the road to jobs and careers that may, for example, pay more money or offer greater and more exciting challenges than in the past.

Take, for example, the word processor who can type 90 words a minute and enjoys working in pleasant surroundings and with mutually supportive individuals. After 10 years of thriving in this type of job where she has really enjoyed using her best skills and abilities, she decides that making $11.00 an hour is not her idea of a swell future; she's definitely not headed for the boardroom with her computer in hand! As her motivation (monetary needs) and career goals change, so too does her need for a different approach to finding a job and changing careers. Self-knowledge generated by the perspective and exercises found in Chapters 7, 8, and 9 may be of limited usefulness as she seeks to break out of her past patterns of motivated abilities and skills.

From Self-Assessment to Self-Transformation

Motivation plays a central role in how and what we choose. When linked to aspirations and positive thinking, motivation can result in major changes in behavior which are largely unpredictable. This approach can and does result in major transformations for many people.

Underlining the concept of MAS is a very conservative notion that one's future behavior will largely be a reflection of one's past patterns of behavior. For some writers, this concept takes on very religious, even messianic, tones of predestination: God hath preordained your patterns when creating the "unique you"; therefore, you can't do much about these patterns other than better understand what they are and then better learn to live with them. This is an interesting and obviously controversial theory which also leads to a conservative view of where one can go from here with his or her life.

A form of historical determinism and probability, the MAS approach is probably valid for 85 percent of the workforce: past patterns of motivated abilities and skills are likely to recur in different work settings and situations. Regardless of what they say or do, most people don't make significant departures from their basic patterns. In fact, most don't even try to make changes since they are content at doing what they always do. However, this approach fails to assist individuals who are highly motivated to break out of their past patterns as they seek to embark on a new future. What, for example, can this approach do for the word processor who wishes to make $100,000 a year and no longer type?

People who are motivated to break out of their past patterns and create a new future need a different approach to jobs and careers. Indeed, self-knowledge based on traditional self-assessment exercises and tests may become an impediment to making future changes. Such information may constrain them from taking new actions that may result in major self-transformations.

Change

Change based on breaking out of old patterns does indeed take place, and it happens more often than we think. And change often begins when an old mind-set is replaced with a new one that rejects such simplistic notions of predestination. It begins when people reject old patterns of thinking, dream the impossible, imagine future states, or set seemingly unrealistic goals for themselves and remain motivated and persist in achieving their goals. A form of breakthrough thinking, this single-minded and determined thinking is demonstrated each year by thousands of people who break out of past patterns of behavior in a process of self-transformation. They make radical departures in their jobs and careers and go on to learn and develop new patterns of motivated abilities and skills. The approaches they use are instructive for our purposes.

> *Self knowledge based on traditional self-assessment may become an impediment to making future changes.*

Breakthrough Thinking

The ability to make major changes in one's patterns of behavior, as well as achieve new goals that may depart significantly from one's past experience, is most closely associated with approaches to entrepreneurship and another school of religion. Such concepts as "the power of positive thinking," "thinking big," "follow your dreams," "shoot for the stars," and "visualizing your future" all have one central element in common—breakthrough thinking centered around setting goals and then developing strategies for achieving those goals. Positive motivations and a "can do" attitude are the most important requirements for this approach. Individuals' goals need not be "realistic" since the notion of being realistic is based upon old patterns of behavior. Such approaches do not encourage individuals to engage in self-assessment. In fact, knowing a great deal about your past may be counter-productive since one of your past patterns might be an *"I can't do it"* attitude of "realism." In other words, you may become paralyzed by your past thinking and behavior patterns. You may not be sufficiently unrealistic to be successful in whatever you do! Therefore, you need to break out of your mental box.

If you want to transcend your past as you seek to acquire a new future, you must approach jobs and careers from a different perspective than identified in earlier chapters. Forget doing a self-assessment that directs you toward your past patterns which is most likely to take you down the *"aha"* road of self-realization. Instead, focus on your interests in relation to new objectives. Just set your goals, develop the proper mind set for achieving those goals (try visualizing), and work like the devil to attain those goals. In so doing, you'll have to maintain a positive attitude and a high level of motivation and energy. Above all, you must be tenacious and persist—despite all odds and disappointments—until you achieve your goals. You must never stop dreaming what may well become a possible dream!

> *Positive motivations and a "can do" attitude are the most important requirements for this approach.*

The Art of Being Unrealistic

This self-transformation approach has numerous and well respected practitioners. Anecdotal, intuitive, and creative in nature, it stresses the importance of **changing your behavior** rather than understanding your behavior. Indeed, the problem is often one's past patterns. The way to solve this problem is to create new patterns of thinking—"break out of the box"—that will lead to success. The power to do this is found within each and every person—the power to condition one's mind to think along new lines.

The techniques of self-transformation are as numerous as the practitioners of this approach. However, they all have some basic elements in common. Not only do they believe in the power of new thinking, but they chart similar strategies for achieving success:

- **Goals:** You must have a clear idea of what you want to do. Get rid of negative thoughts, discard the *"I can't do it"* attitude, and stop procrastinating. You can do anything you want to if only you first change your attitude and set high goals to strive for. Convert your dreams into goals and visualize what you want to achieve. Do not be constrained by your past when setting goals. Your past is likely to be an impediment to your future if you let it interfere with your goals.

- **Planning:** You must transform your goals into a series of action plans that detail how you will go about achieving the goals on a day-to-day basis. If you set goals without a corresponding plan for implementation, you may doom your "big thinking" to frustration and failure. A plan should outline incremental changes in your behavior each day. In the long run such a plan will help create a new "unique you."

- **Discipline:** You must condition yourself to regularly take actions related to your goals and plans. Being single-minded in purpose and being persistent in what you do will be your greatest strengths in achieving your goals.

In the end, individuals are urged to make their behavior consistent with their goals. The mind should stay focused on goals since goals are the driving force for initiating change.

Essentially an individual decision-making approach, it is widely used in many circles to solve just about any problem that is defined as being within the power of individuals to tackle. This approach comes in the same basic form for dealing with a large variety of issues where **motivation** seems to be an important ingredient for initiating change:

> *The mind should stay focused on goals since goals are the driving force for initiating change.*

- increasing personal wealth
- losing weight
- reorganizing personal finances

- motivating salespeople to increase sales
- generating more enthusiasm
- ending procrastination
- improving relationships
- getting better grades

This approach produces a personal form of "snake oil" widely publicized by charismatic motivational speakers, preachers, mentors, and other models who attempt to arouse the masses to take charge of their lives through positive and big thinking. It's the cure-all for almost any problem that you have the power to affect, and that includes almost every problem where you are involved.

Once the major method used by a charismatic school of secular and religious positive thinkers, who still dominate the growing "success" industry of books, videos, and audiocassettes—Napoleon Hill (*Think and Grow Rich*), Anthony Robbins (*Personal Power* and *Unlimited Power*), David Schwartz (*The Magic of Thinking Big*), Zig Ziglar (*How to Get What You Want*), Og Mandino (*Secrets of Success*), Dr. Norman Vincent Peale (*The Power of Positive Thinking*), and Dr. Robert H. Schuller (*You Can Become the Person You Want to Be*)—today this approach is increasingly accepted and respected in business and government circles. Not only have many local insurance and real estate agents been raised on this approach in dealing with people, but many entrepreneurs have been motivated to leave established jobs and careers in pursuit of their business dreams. This approach has yet to make major inroads into career counseling circles where the deterministic and probabilistic MAS approach, with its attendant toolbox of inventories, tests, and one-on-one counseling, remains dominant. However, more and more career writers are trumpeting the power of positive thinking when dealing with issues of self-esteem and approaches to achieving success.

What is especially interesting about this individual-level problem-solving approach is its recent use as a problem-solving approach for organizations. Indeed, many businesses today use this approach to transform their operations in an increasingly competitive environment. Employees are urged to come up with new and innovative strategies and solutions to problems. Instead of analyzing the nature of problems and thus creating what is often termed "paralysis through analysis," they are encouraged to better define and clarify goals and then develop appropriate implementation strategies. An individual problem-solving approach has now come of age as an organizational problem-solving approach. As such, it has moved out of the hands of charismatic success advocates and into the portfolios of management consultants. As an approach to organizational change, this approach takes several forms:

- creative thinking
- brainstorming
- imaging and visualizing
- problem-solving
- breakthrough thinking
- self hypnosis

Research also shows that creative and intuitive people regularly use these methods for solving problems. The writings of William Fezler (***Creative Imagery***) and Gerald Hadler and Shozo Hibino (***Breakthrough Thinking***), which go beyond the anecdotal, have given this approach increased legitimacy for both individuals and organizations.

Learning New Abilities and Skills

The MAS approach to jobs and careers has little to say about education and training since by definition this approach is aimed at uncovering past abilities and skills and then applying them to future jobs by focusing on "transferable skills." However, the self-transformation approach recognizes the importance of acquiring new education and training as part of the process of self-transformation.

Focusing on both goals and the future, the self-transformation approach deals with the issues of education and training relating to one's interests. If, for example, your new thinking specifies being a doctor or lawyer as a career goal, then you must incorporate medical or legal education, training, and certification in your plan of action. In other words, breaking out of your past patterns may mean going back to school where you will acquire new skills, and new ways of thinking, and operate within a new environment for achieving new goals.

Never Settle For Your Past

One thing the self-transformation approach stresses in contrast to the MAS approach is that you should never settle for your past. You can make significant changes if you want to. But you must have clear goals and the necessary motivation to make the changes.

But for many people, change is not what they want. They are

perfectly content at having their future be a reflection of their past MAS patterns. This is what gives their lives stability, predictability, and meaning. For them, the MAS approach is most appropriate. The self-transformation approach especially appeals to risk takers and entrepreneurs.

Our point here is that your future need not be a reflection of your past. If you want more out of life, then you must use an approach that will move you from where you are at present to where you want to be in the future. How your future evolves will in part be determined by the approach you use to shaping that future. At the very least, the approach must deal with motivation and include a plan of action.

Acquiring More Education and Training

Do I have the necessary skills and experience required for the types of jobs that I'm interested in pursuing? How can I improve my present skill levels and acquire more experience? Do I need to learn new skills or be retrained for today's job market? Should I go back to school for a degree, diploma, or certificate? These questions are frequently asked by individuals first entering the job market or those making a job or career change. They will be central questions for individuals who use the self-transformation approach to planning their future. In addition to positive thinking and motivation, they need specific marketable skills desired by employers.

You first need to know what it is you want to do.

It is difficult to provide simple answers to these questions. However, you first need to know what it is you want to do—specify your goals. The next chapter (11) will assist you in doing this. Second, you must conduct research to identify what skills training is really required for particular positions. Notice, we say **skills training**—not education. Although related, there is an important difference between skills training and education. Many employers are looking for specific skills rather than educational credentials. On the other hand, most educational institutions are still oriented toward transferring disciplines and subject matters to students rather than specific skills relevant to the world of work. If you fail to keep these two points in mind, you may waste a great deal of time and money on unnecessary training or seek jobs you are unqualified to perform.

So how should you proceed? Do the necessary self-assessment and data gathering required to answer these questions. Begin by asking yourself a key question for orienting your job search:

"What do I really want to do?"

Once you have a clear idea of your job and career goals, you will be prepared to target your job search toward particular organizations, positions, and individuals.

Assuming you know what you want to do, your next step is to gather information to determine whether you possess the necessary skills to qualify for the job. Obviously, if you are a high school graduate wishing to become a medical doctor, engineer, lawyer, or accountant, you will need several years of highly specialized training for certification in these fields. However, if you want to become an FBI agent, just what educational background, experience, and demonstrated skills do you need? Where do you find this information?

You can begin answering these questions by consulting several publications as suggested in Chapter 12 relevant to conducting a job search. Next, talk to individuals who have a working knowledge of the particular job or career you desire. Contact people in similar positions to what you are seeking. While many educators can be

> *Since many employers prefer conducting their own in-house training, they look for individuals who are motivated, enthusiastic, trainable, and likable.*

helpful, they should rank as a secondary information source. Few educators are objective sources for information about education and training requirements for particular jobs. Remember, most educators are relatively isolated from day-to-day job market realities. Furthermore, educators are in the business of keeping themselves employed by recruiting more students into existing programs as well as by developing new degree and certification programs. They literally "stand where they sit" by promoting more formal education, degrees, and certification—whether or not such training and documentation are really necessary and relevant to the world of work.

If you read materials and talk to informed individuals and employers, you will quickly learn what you need to do to be successful in your job search. If you learn you must return to school for a formal degree or certificate, your information sources will identify the most appropriate type of training you should acquire, as well as recommend where best to receive the training. In many cases you will find you do not need additional training to qualify for a position. Since many employers prefer conducting their own in-house training, they primarily look for individuals who are motivated, enthusiastic, trainable, and likable.

If you must acquire new skills, keep in mind several education and training options available to you:

- Public vocational education
- Private vocational education
- Employer training
- Apprenticeship programs
- Federal employment and training programs
- Armed Forces training
- Home study schools
- Community and junior colleges
- Colleges and universities

Most of these sources emphasize practical hands-on training. Private trade schools, for example, are flourishing—an indication of a shift to practical skills training in education. Each alternative has various advantages and disadvantages, and costs differ considerably.

1. Public vocational education:

Public vocational education is provided through secondary, postsecondary, and adult vocational and technical programs. The emphasis in many secondary schools is to give high school students vocational training in addition to the regular academic program. Postsecondary vocational education is provided for individuals who have left high school but who are not seeking a baccalaureate degree. Adult vocational and technical programs emphasize retraining or upgrading the skills of individuals in the labor force. The traditional agricultural, trade, and industrial emphasis of vocational education has been vastly expanded to include training in distribution, health, home economics, office, and technical occupations. Most programs train individuals for specific occupations, which are outlined in the *Occupational Outlook Handbook*. Each year over 20 million people enroll in public vocational education programs.

2. Noncollegiate postsecondary vocational education:

Nearly 2 million people enroll in over 6,500 noncollegiate post-secondary schools with occupational programs each year. Most of these schools specialize in one of eight vocational areas: cosmetology/barber, business/commercial, trade, hospital, vocational/technical, allied health, arts/design, and technical. They offer programs in seven major areas: agribusiness, marketing and distribution, health, home economics, technical, business and office, and trade and industrial. Over 75 percent of these schools are privately owned institutions. And over 70 percent of the privately owned schools are either cosmetology/barber schools or business and commercial schools. Over 75 percent of the independent nonprofit schools are hospital schools. Over 1 million people complete occupational programs in noncollegiate postsecondary schools each year.

3. Employer training:

Employers spend over $200 billion a year on in-house training and education programs. This training usually involves training new employees, improving employee performance, or preparing employees for new jobs. Skilled and semi-skilled workers are trained through apprenticeship programs, learning-by-doing, and structured on-the-job instruction. Structured classroom training is increasingly offered to skilled workers by in-house trainers, professional associations, private firms, or colleges and universities. Tuition-aid programs are used frequently among firms lacking in-house training capabilities.

4. Apprenticeship programs:

Apprenticeship programs normally range from one to six years, depending on the particular trade and organization. These programs are used most extensively in the trade occupations, especially in construction and metalworking. They involve planned on-the-job training in conjunction with classroom instruction and supervision. Over 500,000 individuals are involved in apprenticeship programs each year. These numbers are likely to increase in the coming decade as America faces an acute shortage of skilled trade workers. Expect apprenticeship programs to expand accordingly.

5. Federal employment and training programs:

Federal employment and training programs largely function through state and local governments. The major federal program is the Workforce Development Act, which recently replaced the Job Training Partnership Act (JTPA) program. The federal government has introduced several new programs within the past seven years such as the School-to-Work and Welfare-to-Work programs as well as One Stop Job Centers. Most of these programs are being increasingly decentralized to the state and local levels.

6. Armed Forces training:

The Armed Forces provide training in numerous occupational skills that may or may not be directly transferred to civilian occupations. Thousands of military recruits complete training programs in several transferable areas each year, such as computer repair, medical care, food service, metalworking, communications, and administration. Occupations unique to the military, such as infantry and guncrew, are less transferable to civilian occupations.

7. Home study (correspondence) schools:

Home study or correspondence schools provide a variety of training options. Most programs concentrate on acquiring a single skill; others may even offer a BA, MA, or Ph.D by mail or over the Internet. Some programs are of questionable quality while others may be revolutionizing the education and training landscape of America. For many people, this is a convenient, inexpensive, and effective way to acquire new skills. Over 5 million people enroll in home study courses each year. Colleges and universities are quickly moving into the home study and distance learning businesses by offering numerous televised and online courses for academic credit. The Public Broadcast System (PBS) offers several home study courses through its Adult Learning Service: computer literacy and applications, basic skills and personal enrichment, sales and customer service, effective communication skills, and management skills.

8. Community and junior colleges:

Community and junior colleges in recent years have broadened their missions from primarily preparing individuals for university degree programs to preparing them with skills for the job market. Accordingly, more of their programs emphasize vocational and occupational curriculums, such as data processing or dental hygiene, which are typically two-year programs resulting in an associate degree. Community and junior colleges will probably continue to expand their programs as they further adjust to the employment needs of communities. Nearly 5 million students enroll in community and junior college programs each year.

9. Colleges and universities:

Colleges and universities continue to provide the traditional four-year and graduate degree programs in various subject fields. While many of the fields are occupational-specific, such as engineering, law, medicine, and business, many other fields are not. The exact relationship of the degree program to the job market varies with different disciplines. As noted earlier, in recent years, graduates of many programs have had difficulty finding employment in their chosen fields. This is particularly true for students who only have a generalist background in the liberal arts. During the past decade many colleges and universities have adjusted to declining enrollments by offering several nontraditional occupational-related courses and programs. Continuing education, special skills training courses, short courses, evening course offerings, distance learning, "telecourses," online courses, and workshops and seminars on job-related matters have become popular with nontraditional, older students who seek specific skills training rather than degrees. At the same time, traditional academic programs are placing greater emphasis on internships and cooperative education programs in order to give students work experience related to their academic programs.

Additional training programs may be sponsored by local governments, professional associations, women's centers, YWCA branches, and religious and civic groups. As training and retraining become more acceptable to the general public, we can expect different forms and types of training programs to be sponsored by various groups.

We also can expect a revolution in the training field, closely related to high-tech developments. Televised education and training courses should continue to increase in number and scope. Computer-based training, similar in some respects to traditional home study programs, will become more prevalent, as computer software and interactive video training packages are developed in response to the new technology and the rising demand for skills training. Much of this training will continue to move online as part of the growing movement toward individualized training. Individuals will be able to quickly access training courses over the Internet to meet their particular skill needs.

Individuals in tomorrow's education training markets will become examples of Toffler's "prosumer society": in a decentralized information market, individuals will choose what training they most desire as well as control when and where they will receive it. With the development of interactive video and computer training programs, individuals will manage the training process in a more efficient and effective manner than with the more centralized, time consuming, and expensive use of traditional student-teacher classroom instruction. This type of training may eventually make many of the previously discussed categories of education and training obsolete.

Become An Informed Consumer

Several resources can help you decide which training path is more appropriate for you. If you use the *Discover II* computerized career planning system, you will find it includes a section that matches education and training programs with career interests. A few other computer programs also match career interests with education and training programs. Contact your local secondary school, community college, or library for information on these programs.

You should begin your search for useful education and training information by consulting several publications. The major sources will be found in the reference section of libraries as well as in guidance offices and career planning centers of schools, colleges, universities, and specialized employment assistance centers. Most of these organizations maintain catalogues, directories, and files listing educational and training opportunities. Impact Publications, for example, has a "School-to-College" catalog that includes a variety of resources on financial aid, educational selection, and educational success.

Two useful sources for information on education and training programs are *Peterson's Guides* and *Barron's Educational Series,* which publish several excellent directories. Most of the directories are updated annually and include basic information on choosing programs and institutions best suited to your interests. Among the many titles offered by Peterson's and Barron's are:

- *Guide to Four-Year Colleges*
- *Guide to Two-Year Colleges*
- *Profiles of American Colleges*
- *The College Money Handbook*
- *Guides to Graduate Study:*
  - *Graduate and Professional Programs*
  - *Humanities, Arts, and Social Sciences*
  - *Biological Sciences*
  - *Physical Sciences, Mathematics, Agricultural Sciences, the Environment and National Resources*
  - *Engineering and Applied Sciences*
  - *Business, Education, Health, Information Studies, Law, and Social Work*
- *Regional Guides to Colleges*
  - *Middle Atlantic States*
  - *Midwest*
  - *New England*
  - *New York*
  - *South*
  - *West*
- *Winning Money For College*

- *How to Prepare for the SAT*
- *Guide to Law Schools*
- *Guide to Graduate Business Schools*
- *Choose a Christian College*
- *Best Buys in College Education*
- *Applying to Colleges and Universities in the United States*
- *Applying to Graduate School in the United States*
- *Competitive Colleges*
- *Colleges With Programs For Students With Learning Disabilities or Attention Deficit Disorders*
- *Distance Learning*
- *Independent Study Catalog*
- *Guide to College Admissions*
- *Corporate Tuition Aid Programs*
- *Graduate Education Directory*

The Princeton Review, College Board, Kaplan, Student Services, Arco, Research and Education Associates, American College Testing, and IDG Books also publish several excellent directories on educational institutions, testing, and finance. Many of these directories include software for searching their databases and developing educational strategies.

Most major libraries have copies of these publications in their reference section. If you cannot find them in your local library, check with your local bookstore or contact the publishers directly or request Impact Publication's comprehensive catalog to these resources (Tel. 703-361-7300).

If you decide you need to acquire a specific skill, consult various professional or trade associations; many can provide you with a list of reputable institutions offering skills training in particular fields. The names, addresses, and telephone numbers of all major associations are listed in the *Encyclopedia of Associations* (Gale Research) and *National Trade and Professional Associations* (Columbia Books), two extremely useful directories found in the reference section of most libraries. Most associations have websites which include information on their membership and services. You can easily locate these associations by using such search engines as Google.com and iWon.com.

The U.S. Department of Labor's *Occupational Outlook Handbook* also lists useful names, addresses, and websites relating to employment training in specific fields. Consult the *"Sources of Career Information"* section in the latest edition of this biannual directory. This book also is available in most libraries, online (*http://stats.bls.gov/ocohome.htm*), or can be purchased from Impact Publications by completing the order form at the end of this book or online: *www.impactpublications.com.*

For information on **private trade and technical schools,** be sure to get a copy of the ***Handbook of Accredited Private Trade and Technical Schools*** which is distributed by the Career College Association, 750 1st St., NE., Washington, DC 20002 (Tel. 202/336-6700).

For information on **apprenticeship programs**, get a copy of *The National Apprenticeship Program and Apprenticeship Information* through the Bureau of Apprenticeships and Training (BAT), U.S. Department of Labor, 200 Constitution Ave., NW, Room N-4649, Washington, DC 20210 (Tel. 202/219-5921). BAT offices are also found in each state. To find if there is a BAT office near you, consult the White or Blue Pages of your telephone directory under *"United States Government—Department of Labor."* Your local library and public employment service office should also have information on apprenticeship programs.

If you are interested in **home study and correspondence courses**, contact the National Home Study Council (NHSC) for information on home study programs. NHSC distributes copies of a useful publication entitled ***Directory of Accredited Home Study Programs***. For information on this and other NHSC publications, contact: National Home Study Council, 1601 18th St., NW, Washington, DC 20009 (Tel. 202/234-5100).

You also need to determine the quality and suitability of these education and training programs. Many programs have reputations for fraud, abuse, and incompetence—primarily taking your time and money in exchange for broken promises. After all, this is a business transaction—your money in exchange for their services. As an informed consumer, you must demand quality performance for your money. Therefore, when contacting a particular institution, ask to speak to former students and graduates. Write to the Council on Postsecondary Accreditation (One Dupont Circle, Suite 760, Washington, DC 20036) to inquire about the school's credentials. Focus your attention on the *results* or *outcomes* the institution achieves. Instead of asking workload questions —how many faculty have Master's or Ph.D degrees, or how many students are enrolled—ask these performance or outcome questions:

- What are last year's graduates doing today?
- Where do they work and for whom?
- How much do they earn?
- How many were placed in jobs through this institution?

Institutions that can answer these questions focus on *performance.* Beware of those that can't answer these questions, for they may not be doing an adequate job to meet your needs.

Most colleges and universities will provide assistance to adult learners. Contact student services, continuing education, academic advising, adult services, or women's offices at your local community college, college, or university. Be sure to talk to present and former students about the ***expectations and results*** of the programs for them. Always remember that educators are first in the business of keeping themselves employed and, second, in the business of delivering educational services. And today, more than ever, educational institutions need students to keep their programs alive. Don't necessarily expect professional educators to be objective about your future vis-a-vis their interests, skills, and programs. At the very least, you must do a critical evaluation of their programs and services.

> *Thoroughly research education and training alternatives before you invest any money, time, or effort.*

Other useful sources of information on education and training programs are your telephone book and employers. Look under "Schools" in the Yellow Pages of your telephone directory. Call the schools and ask them to send you literature and application forms and discuss the relevance of their programs to the job market. You should also talk to employers and individuals who have work experience in the field that interests you. Ask them how best to acquire the necessary skills for particular occupations. Most important, thoroughly research education and training alternatives before you invest any money, time, or effort.

Know How to Finance Your Future

Most people can take advantage of training opportunities in order to better function in today's job market. Lack of information and money are often excuses based upon ignorance of available resources and costs.

Education and training may not be cheap, but neither need they be excessively expensive. It is best to view education and training as good investments in your future.

You will find many alternatives to expensive training. For example, adult education programs sponsored by the public school system and community colleges are relatively inexpensive to attend. If you have the will, you usually can find the way in the U.S. education and training systems.

Financial aid for education and training is somewhat bewildering and confusing. It requires research and perseverance on your part. You should begin by contacting the financial aid officers at various institutions that offer the training you desire for advice on financial aid. The particular institutions as well as many other organizations provide scholarships, fellowships, grants, loans, and work-study programs. The American Legion, for example, publishes a useful booklet—*Need a Lift?*—on careers and scholarships for undergraduate and graduate students. To get a single free copy, call 317/630-1200 or write to: American Legion, ATTN: National Emblem Sales, 700 N. Pennsylvania St., P.O. Box 1055, Indianapolis, IN 46204. The College Board also publishes information on student aid. Among its many publications is its annual *Meeting College Costs*. For information on this and other College Board publications, contact: College Board Publications, Box 886, New York, NY 10101. You'll also find numerous scholarship directories available in bookstores and libraries. The most comprehensive such directories are published by Peterson's, Barron's, Kaplan, Gale Research, Student Services, and Cassidy. Most are available through Impact Publications (request their "School-to-College" catalog).

Information on federal government financial aid programs—grants, loans, work-study, and benefits—can be obtained by writing to the U.S. Department of Education for a pamphlet entitled *The Student Guide to Federal Financial Aid Programs*. Revised yearly, this publication can be obtained by calling or writing to: Federal Student Aid Programs, P.O. Box 84, Washington, DC 20044, or call 800/433-3243.

For information on financial assistance for specific groups, such as Hispanics, blacks, Native Americans, and women, get a copy of the U.S. Department of Education's *Higher Education Opportunities For Minorities and Women* (Superintendent of Documents, U.S. Government Printing Office, Washington, DC 20402, Tel. 202/783-3238 for order information). You should also consider examining three useful resources published by Ferguson (previous editions published by Garrett Park Press) relevant to minorities:

- *The Big Book of Minority Opportunities*, Willis L. Johnson (ed.), (Chicago: Ferguson)

- *Financial Aid For Minority Students* (a series of booklets on Allied Health, Business, Education, Engineering, Law, Journalism/Communications, Medicine, Science), Ruth V. Swann (ed.), (Chicago: Ferguson)

- *The National Directory of Minority Organizations*, Katherine W. Cole (ed.) (Chicago: Ferguson)

Student Services, Inc., also publishes a useful scholarship directory for ethnic and religious minorities as well as women and people with disabilities: *The Minority Student's Complete Scholarship Book* (Sourcebooks). Also look for Barry Beckman's two guides for black students: *The Black Students Guide to Colleges* and *The Black Student's Guide to Scholarships* (Madison Books). Gale Research publishes a series of directories on four minority groups: Asian Americans, Black Americans, Hispanic Americans, and Native Americans. These books can be ordered directly from Impact Publications by completing the order information at the end of this book or through their website: *www.impactpublications.com*.

Compare Costs and Performance Options

Don't forget to compare the different costs of various educational and training programs. Many are inexpensive whereas others are extremely costly. Keep in mind that there is no necessary correlation between educational costs and performance; you may well get your best performance at the lowest cost and the worst performance at the highest cost—and vice versa. Indeed, one of the major characteristics of the American education and training system is the variety of *options* it offers individuals. These include different choices in terms of programs, quality, costs, and expected outcomes. You must do research in order to identify relevant options and make informed choices.

Beware of Myths

Beware of education and training myths. Additional education and training are not always the answer for entry or advancement within the job market. Remember, education is a big $400-billion a year business. Exhibiting a great deal of inertia, few educational institutions are prepared to describe their performance in relation to today's job market. At best, educational institutions are most adept at keeping their businesses well and alive through the marketing of degree programs to relatively uninformed, accepting, and compliant consumers.

Contrary to what educators may tell you, additional education and training may not be necessary for entering or advancing within today's job market. But it is a good investment for the job markets of tomorrow. To determine if you need additional education and training, you should first learn what it is you do well and enjoy doing (through self-assessment) and then identify what it is you need to do to get what you want (through research). Education and training may be only one of several things you need to do. You may, for example, determine that you need to change your behavior by setting goals, becoming more focused on achieving results, and improving your dress and appearance. Or you may need to develop effective job search skills as well as relocate to a new community. After all, employers spend more than $200 billion each year on employee training and retraining—much of which is spent because of the failure of traditional educational institutions.

You may learn it is best to find an apprenticeship program or get into a particular organization that provides excellent training for its employees. Such training will be both up-to-date and relevant to the job market. Most of the best run corporations rely on their own in-house training rather than on institutions outside the corporation. When making hiring decisions, such organizations may be more concerned with your overall level of intelligence as reflected in your ability to learn, acquire new skills, and grow within the organization than with the specific work-content skills you initially bring to the job.

11

Set Goals and Specify
Your Objective

ONCE YOU IDENTIFY YOUR INTERESTS, SKILLS, AND abilities, you should be well prepared to develop a clear and purposeful objective for targeting your job search toward specific organizations and employers. With a renewed sense of direction and versed in an appropriate language, you should be able to communicate to employers that you are a talented and purposeful individual who *achieves results.* Your objective must tell employers what you will *do for them* rather than what you want from them. It targets your accomplishments around employers' needs. In other words, your objective should be employer-centered rather than self-centered.

Goals and Objectives

Goals and objectives are statements of what you want to do in the future. When combined with an assessment of your interests, values, abilities and skills and related to specific jobs, they give your job search needed direction and meaning for the purpose of targeting specific employers. Without them, your job search may founder as you present an image of uncertainty and confusion to potential employers.

When you identify your strengths, you also create the necessary database and vocabulary for developing your job objective. Using this vocabulary, you should be able to communicate to employers that you are a talented and purposeful individual who achieves results.

If you fail to do the preliminary self-assessment work necessary for developing a clear objective, you will probably wander aimlessly in a highly decentralized, fragmented, and chaotic job market looking for interesting jobs you might fit into. Your goal, instead, should be to find a job or career that is compatible with your interests, motivations, skills, and talents as well as related to a vision of your future. In short, try to find a job fit for you and your future rather than try to fit into a job that happens to be advertised and for which you think you can qualify.

Examine Your Past, Present, and Future

Depending on how you approach your job search, your goals can be largely a restatement of your past MAS patterns or a vision of your future. If you base your job search on an analysis of your motivated abilities and skills, you may prefer restating your past patterns as your present and future goals. On the other hand, you may want to establish a vision of your future and set goals that motivate you to achieve that vision through self-transformation.

> *Your objective should be employer- rather than self-centered. It should reflect your honesty and integrity; it should not be "hyped."*

The type of goals you choose to establish will involve different processes. However, the strongest goals will be those that combine your motivated abilities and skills with a realistic vision of your future.

Orient Yourself to Employers' Needs

Your objective should be a concise statement of what you want to do and what you have to offer to an employer. The position you seek is "what you want to do"; your qualifications are "what you have to offer." Your objective should state your strongest qualifications for meeting employers' needs. It should communicate what you have to offer an employer without emphasizing what you expect the employer to do for you. In other words, your objective should be *work-centered*, not self-centered; it should not contain trite terms which emphasize what you want, such as give me a(n) "opportunity for advancement," "position working with people," "progressive company," or "creative position." Such terms are viewed as "canned" job search language which say little of value about you. Above all, your objective should reflect your honesty and integrity; it should not be *"hyped."*

Identifying what it is you want to do can be one of the most difficult job search tasks. Indeed, most job hunters lack clear objectives. Many engage in a random, and somewhat mindless, search for jobs by identifying available job opportunities and then adjusting their skills and objectives to fit specific job openings. While you can get a job using this approach, you may be misplaced and unhappy with what you find. You will fit into a job rather than find a job that is fit for you.

Knowing what you want to do can have numerous benefits. First, you define the job market rather than let it define you. The inherent fragmentation and chaos of the job market should be advantageous for you, because it enables you to systematically organize job opportunities around your specific objectives and skills. Second, you will communicate professionalism to prospective employers. They will receive a precise indication of your interests, qualifications, and purposes, which places you ahead of most other applicants. Third, being purposeful means being able to communicate to employers what you want to do. Employers are not interested in hiring indecisive and confused individuals. They want to know what it is you can do for them. With a clear objective, based upon a thorough understanding of your MAS, you can take control of the situation.

> *The strongest goals will be those that combine your motivated abilities and skills with a realistic vision of your future.*

Finally, few employers really know what they want in a candidate. Like most job seekers, employers lack clear employment objectives and knowledge about how the job market operates. If you know what you want, you can help the employer define his "needs" as your objective.

Be Purposeful and Realistic

Your objective should communicate that you are a *purposeful individual who achieves results.* It can be stated over different time periods as well as at various levels of abstraction and specificity. You can identify short, intermediate, and long-range objectives and general to specific objectives. Whatever the case, it is best to know your prospective audience before deciding on the type of objective. Your objective should reflect your career interests as well as employers' needs.

Objectives also should be *realistic.* You may want to become President. However, this objective is probably unrealistic. While it may represent your dream, you need to be more realistic in terms of what you can personally accomplish in the immediate future. What, for example, are you prepared to deliver to prospective employers over the next few months? Refine your objective by thinking about the next major step or two you would like to make in your career advancement—not some grandiose leap outside reality!

Project Yourself Into the Future

Even after identifying your abilities and skills, specifying an objective can be the most difficult and tedious step in the job search process; it can stall the resume writing process indefinitely. This simple one-sentence, 25-word statement can take days or weeks to formulate and clearly define. Yet, it must be specified prior to writing the resume and engaging in other job search steps. An objective gives meaning and direction to all other activities.

Your objective should be viewed as a function of several influences. Since you want to build upon your strengths and you want to be realistic, your abilities and skills will play a central role in formulating your work objective. At the same time, you do not want your objective to become a function solely of your past accomplishments and skills. You may be very skilled in certain areas, but you may not want to use these skills in the future. As a result, your values and interests filter which skills you will or will not incorporate into your work objective.

Overcoming the problem of historical determinism—your future merely reflecting your past—requires incorporating additional components into defining your objective. One of the most important is your ideals, fantasies, or dreams. Everyone engages in these, and sometimes they come true. These may include making $1,000,000 by age 40; owning a Mercedes-Benz; taking a trip to Rome; owning a business; developing financial independence; writing a best-selling novel; solving major social problems; or winning the Nobel Peace Prize. If your fantasies require more money than you are now making, you will need to incorporate monetary considerations into your work objective. For example, if you have these fantasies, but your sense of realism tells you that your objective is to move from a $40,000 a year position to a $42,000 a year position, you will be going nowhere, unless you can fast-track in your new position. Therefore, you will need to set a higher objective to satisfy your fantasies.

You can develop realistic objectives many different ways. Our approach is designed to provide you with sufficient corroborating data from several sources and perspectives so that you can make preliminary decisions. If you follow our steps in setting a realistic objective, you should be able to give your job search clear direction.

Four major steps are involved in developing a work objective. Each step can be implemented in a variety of ways:

STEP 1: Develop or obtain basic data on your functional/transferable skills, which we discussed in Chapter 7.

STEP 2: Acquire corroborating data about yourself from others, tests, and yourself. Try these resources:

A.   **From others:** Ask three to five individuals whom you know well to evaluate you according to the questions in the "Strength Evaluation" form on page 129. Explain to these people that you believe their candid appraisal will help you gain a better understanding of your strengths and weaknesses from the perspectives of others. Ask them to complete and return it to a designated third party who will share the information—but not the respondent's name—with you.

B.   **From vocational tests:** Although we prefer self-generated data, vocationally-oriented tests can help clarify, confirm, and translate your understanding of yourself into occupational directions. It's best to contact a professional career counselor who can administer and interpret the tests. We suggest several of the following:

- *Myers-Briggs Type Indicator®*
- *Strong Interest Inventory*
- *Edwards Personal Preference Schedule*
- *Kuder Occupational Interest Survey*
- *Jackson Vocational Interest Survey*

Strength Evaluation

TO: _____

FROM: _____

I am going through a career assessment process and thought you would be an appropriate person to ask for assistance. Would you please candidly respond to the questions below? Your comments will be given to me by the individual designed below; s/he will not reveal your name. Your comments will be used for advising purposes only. Thank you.

What are my strengths?

What weak areas might I need to improve?

In your opinion, what do I need in a job or career to make me satisfied?

Please return to: _____

- *Vocational Interest Inventory*
- *Career Assessment Inventory*
- *Temperament and Values Inventory*

C. **From yourself:** Numerous alternatives are available for you
    to practice redundancy. Refer to the exercises in Chapter 8
    that assist you in identifying your work values, job frustra-
    tions, things you love to do, things you enjoy most about
    work, and your preferred interpersonal environments.

**STEP 3: Project your values and preferences into the future
by completing simulation and creative thinking exercises:**

A. **Ten Million Dollar Exercise:** First, assume that you are
    given a $10,000,000 gift; now you don't have to work. Since
    the gift is restricted to your use only, you cannot give any
    part of it away. What will you do with your time! At first?
    Later on? Second, assume that you are given another
    $10,000,000, but this time you are required to give it all
    away. What kinds of causes, organizations, charities, etc.
    would you support? Answer these questions:

What Will I Do With Two $10,000,000 Gifts?

First gift is restricted to my use only:

_____

_____

_____

_____

Second gift must be given away:

_____

_____

_____

_____

B. **Obituary Exercise:** Make a list of the most important things you would like to do or accomplish before you die. Two alternatives are available for doing this. First, make a list in response to this lead-in statement: "Before I die, I want to..."

Before I Die, I Want to . . .

1. _____
   _____

2. _____
   _____

3. _____
   _____

4. _____
   _____

5. _____
   _____

6. _____
   _____

7. _____
   _____

8. _____
   _____

9. _____
   _____

10. _____
    _____

Second, write a newspaper article which is actually your obituary for 10 years from now. Stress your accomplishments over the coming 10-year period.

My Obituary

Obituary for Mr./Ms. _____ to appear in the _____ newspaper in 2011.

_____

_____

_____

_____

_____

_____

_____

_____

_____

_____

_____

C. **My Ideal Work Week:** Starting with Monday, place each day of the week as the headings of seven sheets of paper. Develop a daily calendar with 30-minute intervals, beginning at 7am and ending at midnight. Your calendar should consist of a 118-hour week. Next, beginning at 7am on Monday (sheet one), identify the *ideal activities* you would enjoy doing, or need to do for each 30-minute segment during the day. Assume you are capable of doing anything; you have no constraints except those you impose on yourself. Furthermore, assume that your work schedule consists of 40 hours per week. How will you fill your time? Be specific.

My Ideal Work Week

Monday
am

7:00 _____	4:00 _____
7:30 _____	4:30 _____
8:00 _____	5:00 _____
10:30 _____	5:30 _____
11:00 _____	6:00 _____
11:30 _____	6:30 _____
12:00 _____	7:00 _____
p.m.	7:30 _____
1:00 _____	8:00 _____
1:30 _____	8:30 _____
2:00 _____	9:00 _____
2:30 _____	9:30 _____
3:00 _____	10:00 _____
1:00 _____	10:30 _____
1:30 _____	11:00 _____
2:00 _____	11:30 _____
2:30 _____	12:00 _____
3:00 _____	Continue for Tuesday–Friday
3:30 _____	

D.   My Ideal Job Description: Develop your ideal future job. Be sure you include:

- Specific interests you want to build into your job.
- Work responsibilities.
- Working conditions.
- Earnings and benefits.

- Interpersonal environment.
- Working circumstances, opportunities, and goals.

Use "My Ideal Job Specifications" on page 135 to outline your ideal job. After completing this exercise, synthesize the job and write a detailed paragraph which describes the kind of job you would most enjoy:

Description of My Ideal Job

_____

_____

_____

_____

_____

_____

_____

_____

_____

_____

STEP 4: Test your objective against reality. Evaluate and refine it by conducting market research, a force field analysis, library research, and informational interviews.

A. **Market Research:** Four steps are involved in conducting this research:

   1. **Products or services:** Based upon all other assessment activities, make a list of what you *do* or *make* (go to page 136):

My Ideal Job Specifications

Job Interests	Work Responsibilities	Working Conditions	Earnings/ Benefits	Interpersonal Environment	Circumstances/ Opportunities/ Goals

Products/Services I Do or Make

1. _____

2. _____

3. _____

4. _____

5. _____

6. _____

7. _____

8. _____

9. _____

10. _____

2. **Market:** Identify who needs, wants, or buys what you do or make. Be specific. Include individuals, groups, and organizations. Then, identify *what* specific *needs* your products or services fill. Next, assess the *results* you achieve with your products or services.

The Market For My Products/Services

Individuals, groups, organizations needing me:

1. _____

2. _____

3. _____

4. _____

5. _____

Needs I fulfill:

1. _____

2. _____

3. _____

4. _____

5. _____

Results/outcomes/impacts of my products/services:

1. _____

2. _____

3. _____

4. _____

5. _____

3. **New Markets:** Brainstorm a list of *who else* needs your products or services. Think about ways of expanding your market. Next, list any new needs your current or new market has which you might be able to fill:

Developing New Needs

Who else needs my products/services?

1. _____

2. _____

3. _____

4. _____

5. _____

New ways to expand my market:

1. _____

2. _____

3. _____

4. _____

5. _____

New needs I should fulfill:

1. _____
2. _____
3. _____
4. _____
5. _____

4. **New products and/or services:** List any new products or services you can offer and any new needs
   you can satisfy:

New Products/Services I Can Offer

1. _____
2. _____
3. _____
4. _____
5. _____

New Needs I Can Meet

1. _____
2. _____
3. _____
4. _____
5. _____

B. **Force Field Analysis:** Once you have developed a tenta-
    tive or firm objective, force field analysis can help you
    understand the various internal and external forces affecting
    the achievement of your objective. Force field analysis
    follows a specific sequence of activities:

    ■ Clearly state your objective or course of action.

- List the positive and negative forces affecting your objective. Specify the internal and external forces working *for* and *against* you in terms of who, what, where, when, and how much. Estimate the impact of each force upon your objective.

- Analyze the forces. Assess the importance of each force upon your objective and its probable effect upon you. Some forces may be irrelevant to your goal. You may need additional information to make a thorough analysis.

- Maximize positive forces and minimize negative ones. Identify actions you can take to strengthen positive forces and to neutralize, overcome, or reverse negative forces. Focus on real, important, and probable key forces.

- Assess the feasibility of attaining your objective and, if necessary, modifying it in light of new information.

C. **Conduct Library and Online Research:** This research should strengthen and clarify your objective. Consult various reference materials on alternative jobs and careers. Most of these resources are available in print form at your local or college library. Some are available in electronic versions online. If you explore the numerous company profiles and career sites available on the Internet (start with *www.Hoovers.com* and *www.Vault.com*), you should be able to tap into a wealth of information on alternative jobs, careers, and employers. One of the best resources for initiating online research is Margaret Riley Dikel and Frances Roehm's *The Guide to Internet Job Searching* (Lincolnwood, IL: NTC Publishing, 2000). We identify many of the major employment sites on the World Wide Web in Chapter 15 (see pages 179-180).

Career and Job Alternatives

- *Encyclopedia of Careers and Vocational Guidance*
- *Enhanced Guide For Occupational Exploration*
- *Guide For Occupational Exploration*

- *Occupational Outlook Handbook*
- *Occupational Outlook Quarterly*
- *O*NET Dictionary of Occupational Titles*

Industrial Directories

- *Dun and Bradstreet's Middle Market Directory*
- *Dun and Bradstreet's Million Dollar Directory*
- *Encyclopedia of Business Information Sources*
- *Geography Index*
- *Moody's Industrial Directory*
- *Poor's Register of Corporations, Directors, and Executives*
- *Standard and Poor's Industrial Index*
- *Standard and Poor's Register of Corporations*
- *Standard Rate & Data Business Publications*
- *Thomas' Register of American Manufacturers*
- *Ward's Business Directory*

Associations

- *Encyclopedia of Associations*
- *National Trade and Professional Associations*

Government Sources

- *The Book of the States*
- *Congressional Directory*
- *Congressional Staff Directory*
- *Congressional Yellow Book*
- *Federal Directory*
- *Federal Yellow Book*
- *Municipal Yearbook*
- *Taylor's Encyclopedia of Government Officials*
- *United Nations Yearbook*
- *United States Government Manual*
- *Washington Information Directory*

Newspapers

- *The Wall Street Journal*
- Major city newspapers
- Trade newspapers
- Any city newspaper—especially the Sunday edition.

Business Publications

- *Barron's, Business Week, Fast Company, Forbes, Fortune, Harvard Business Review, Time, Newsweek, Economist*
- Annual issues of publications surveying the best jobs for the year: *Money, Working Women, U.S. News & World Report*

Other Library Resources

- Trade journals (refer to the *Directory of Special Libraries and Information Centers* and *Subject Collections: A Guide to Specialized Libraries of Businesses, Governments, and Associations*).
- Publications of Chambers of Commerce; State Manufacturing Associations; and federal, state, and local government agencies
- Telephone books—The Yellow Pages
- Trade books on "How to get a job"

4. **Conduct Informational Interviews:** This may be the most useful way to clarify and refine your objective. We'll discuss this procedure in the next chapter.

After completing these steps, you will have identified what it is you *can* do (abilities and skills), enlarged your thinking to include what it is you would *like* to do (aspirations), and probed the realities of implementing your objective. Thus, setting a realistic work objective is a function of the diverse considerations represented on page 142.

Objective Setting Process

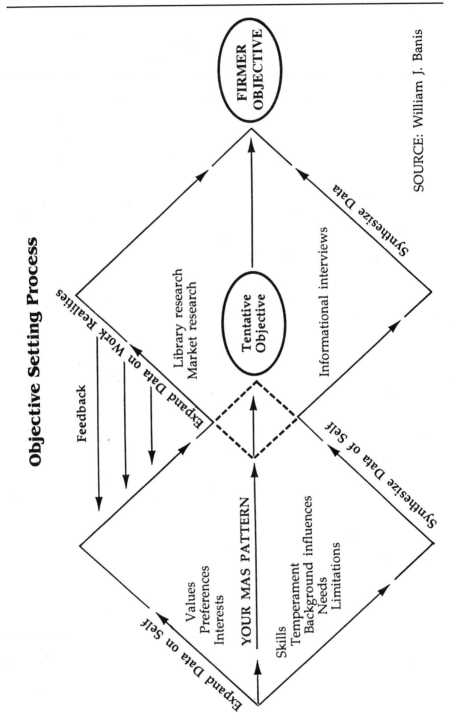

SOURCE: William J. Banis

Your work objective is a function of both subjective and objective information as well as idealism and realism. We believe you should place the strongest emphasis on your competencies as well as include a broad database. Your work objective is realistic in that it is tempered by your past experiences, accomplishments, skills, and current research. An objective formulated in this manner permits you to think beyond your past experiences.

State a Functional Objective

Your job objective should be oriented toward skills and results or outcomes. You can begin by stating a functional job objective at two different levels: a general objective and a specific one for communicating your qualifications to employers both on resumes and in interviews. Thus, this objective-setting process sets the stage for other key job search activities. For the general objective, begin with the statement:

Stating Your General Objective

I would like a job where I can use my ability to _____
skill

which will result in _____.
outcome

The objective in this statement is both a *skill* and an *outcome.* For example, you might state:

Skills-Based and Results-Oriented Objective

I would like a job where my experience in program development, supported by innovative decision-making and systems engineering abilities, will result in an expanded clientele and a more profitable organization.

At a second level you may wish to re-write this objective in order to target it at various consulting firms. For example, on your resume it becomes:

Job-Targeted Objective

An increasingly responsible research position in consulting, where proven decision-making and system engineering abilities will be used for improving organizational productivity.

The following are examples of weak and strong objective statements. Various styles are also presented:

Weak Objectives

Management position which will use business administration degree and will provide opportunities for rapid advancement.

A position in social services which will allow me to work with people in a helping capacity.

A position in Personnel Administration with a progressive firm.

Sales Representative with opportunity for advancement.

Stronger Objectives

To use computer science training in software development for designing and implementing operating systems.

A public relations position which will maximize opportunities to develop and implement programs, to organize people and events, and to communicate positive ideas and images. Effective in public speaking and in managing a publicity/promotional campaign.

A position as a General Sales Representative with a pharmaceutical house which will use chemistry background and ability to work on a self-directed basis in managing a marketing territory.

A position in data analysis where skills in mathematics, computer programming, and deductive reasoning will contribute to new systems development.

Retail Management position which will use sales/customer service experience and creative abilities for product display and merchandising. Long term goal: Progression to merchandise manager with corporate-wide responsibilities for product line.

Responsible position in investment research and analysis. Interests and skills include securities analysis, financial planning, and portfolio management. Long range goal: to become a Chartered Financial Analyst.

It is important to relate your objective to your audience. While you definitely want a good job, your audience wants to know what you can do for them. Remember, your objective should be work-centered, not self-centered.

12

Alternative Jobs and Careers

ONCE YOU HAVE A CLEAR IDEA OF WHAT YOU DO well and enjoy doing, as well as what you would like to do in the future, you need to link this information on yourself to the world of work. For in the end, you need to know what jobs are most appropriate for someone with your "qualifications." You do this through a combination of investigative techniques that put you close to the real world of work and employers.

Linkage Systems

There are no magical formulas for relating information on yourself to specific jobs. While some employment specialists have attempted to develop elaborate systems that relate individual personality, interests, values, abilities, skills, and objectives to different job titles, most such efforts are highly generalized. At best they give you a general overview of the types of jobs you might be most interested in pursuing. Few provide you with the detailed information necessary for making informed career decisions.

Nonetheless, you should examine some of these systems for the purpose of narrowing your job choices to a manageable whole for further investigation. They come in many forms, from simple checklists for matching individual characteristics to job titles to more intensive forms of content analysis requiring a high level of analytical skills along with information on specific jobs. The U.S. Department of Labor, for example, has devised a job-matching chart that relates information on the individual to nearly 200 of the most popular and rapidly growing jobs in the United States. The jobs are clustered into related occupational areas as illustrated on pages 148-154. Further information on these and other related jobs is found in two of the Department of Labor's most widely used occupational reference works: *Occupational Outlook Handbook* and *O*NET Dictionary of Occupational Titles*. Both books are available through Impact Publications.

The *Guide For Occupational Exploration* also attempts to relate information on individuals to specific occupational fields. Focusing primarily on individual interests, but also including skills and abilities, the *Guide* identifies numerous jobs outlined in the *Dictionary of Occupational Titles* and relates these to information on individuals. This ambitious attempt to relate the descriptive nature of the *Dictionary* relevant to individual interests and skills provides a wealth of information on jobs. For individual occupations, it includes numerous checklists that help individuals focus on the interests, skills, abilities, and educational training required for each job.

Less ambitious and more eclectic systems are occasionally developed by enterprising writers and employment specialists. One of the most popular ones is outlined in Barry and Linda Gale's book, *Discover What You're Best At*. Dubbed the *"National Career Aptitude System,"* the author's so-called "system" is a series of self-administered multiple choice tests that examine business, clerical, logical, mechanical, numerical, and social aptitudes. These, in turn, are clustered and then related to some very general occupational titles. The book also includes brief descriptions of more than 1,100 careers which are also found in the *Dictionary of Occupational Titles* and the *Occupational Outlook Handbook*. The latest edition of this book assigns occupational cluster codes to each occupational description.

Practitioners of the motivated abilities and skills approach to career discovery also stress the importance of related self-assessment information to specific jobs. One of the most explicit and labor-intensive approaches is outlined in Miller and Mattson's *The Truth About You*. Their analytical method, trademarked as the SIMA technique for assessing motivated abilities, is also used for "matching" one's motivated abilities with specific jobs. This requires identifying the motivational patterns associated with specific jobs and then fitting one's

DEPARTMENT OF LABOR JOB MATCHING SYSTEM

	Job requirements								Work environment			Occupational characteristics					
	1. Leadership/persuasion	2. Helping/instructing others	3. Problem-solving/creativity	4. Initiative	5. Work as part of a team	6. Frequent public contact	7. Manual dexterity	8. Physical stamina	9. Hazardous	10. Outdoors	11. Confined	12. Geographically concentrated	13. Part-time	14. Earnings	15. Employment growth	16 Number of new jobs through 1995 (in thousands)	17. Entry requirements
Executive, Administrative, and Managerial Occupations																	
Managers and Administrators																	
Bank officers and managers	•	•	•	•	•	•					•			H	H	119	H
Health services managers	•	•	•	•	•	•								H	H	147	H
Hotel managers and assistants	•	•	•	•	•	•								[1]	H	21	M
School principals and assistant principals	•	•	•	•	•	•								H	L	12	H
Management Support Occupations																	
Accountants and auditors		•	•		•	•					•			H	H	307	H
Construction and building inspectors		•	•	•	•		•			•				M	L	4	M
Inspectors and compliance officers, except construction		•	•	•	•		•			•				H	L	10	M
Personnel, training, and labor relations specialists	•	•	•	•	•	•								H	M	34	H
Purchasing agents	•		•		•	•								H	M	36	H
Underwriters			•											H	H	17	H
Wholesale and retail buyers	•	•	•	•	•									M	M	28	H
Engineers, Surveyors, and Architects																	
Architects			•	•	•	•	•							H	H	25	H
Surveyors	•				•		•	•		•				M	M	6	M
Engineers																	
Aerospace engineers			•	•	•							•		H	H	14	H
Chemical engineers			•	•	•									H	H	13	H
Civil engineers			•	•	•									H	H	46	H
Electrical and electronics engineers			•	•	•									H	H	206	H
Industrial engineers			•	•	•									H	H	37	H
Mechanical engineers			•	•	•									H	H	81	H
Metallurgical, ceramics, and materials engineers			•	•	•									H	H	4	H
Mining engineers			•	•	•									H	L	[2]	H
Nuclear engineers			•	•	•									H	L	1	H
Petroleum engineers			•	•	•							•		H	M	4	H
Natural Scientists and Mathematicians																	
Computer and Mathematical Occupations																	
Actuaries			•	•							•	•		H	H	4	H
Computer systems analysts	•	•	•	•	•						•			H	H	212	H
Mathematicians			•	•										H	M	4	H
Statisticians			•	•										H	M	4	H

[1] Estimates not available.
[2] Less than 500.

	Job requirements											Work environment		Occupational characteristics			
	1. Leadership/persuasion	2. Helping/instructing others	3. Problem-solving/creativity	4. Initiative	5. Work as part of a team	6. Frequent public contact	7. Manual dexterity	8. Physical stamina	9. Hazardous	10. Outdoors	11. Confined	12. Geographically concentrated	13. Part-time	14. Earnings	15. Employment growth	16. Number of new jobs through 1995 (in thousands)	17. Entry requirements
Physical Scientists			•	•										H	M		H
Chemists			•	•										H	L	9	H
Geologists and geophysicists			•	•	•				•			•		H	M	7	H
Meteorologists			•	•	•									H	M	1	H
Physicists and astronomers			•	•										H	L	2	H
Life Scientists																	
Agricultural scientists			•	•										'	M	3	H
Biological scientists			•	•										H	M	10	H
Foresters and conservation scientists	•		•	•	•			•	•	•				H	L	2	H
Social Scientists, Social Workers, Religious Workers, and Lawyers																	
Lawyers	•	•	•	•	•	•								H	H	174	H
Social Scientists and Urban Planners																	
Economists			•	•										H	M	7	H
Psychologists		•	•	•		•								H	H	21	H
Sociologists			•	•		•								H	L	'	H
Urban and regional planners	•		•	•	•	•								H	L	2	H
Social and Recreation Workers																	
Social workers	•	•	•	•	•	•								M	H	75	H
Recreation workers	•	•	•	•	•	•	•	•		•			•	L	H	26	M
Religious Workers																	
Protestant ministers	•	•	•	•	•	•								L	'	'	H
Rabbis	•	•	•	•	•	•								H	'	'	H
Roman Catholic priests	•	•	•	•	•	•								L	'	'	H
Teachers, Counselors, Librarians, and Archivists																	
Kindergarten and elementary school teachers	•	•	•	•	•	•	•	•						M	H	281	H
Secondary school teachers	•	•	•	•	•	•		•						M	L	48	H
Adult and vocational education teachers	•	•	•	•	•	•	•	•					•	M	M	48	H
College and university faculty	•	•	•	•	•	•		•	°				•	H	L	−77	H
Counselors	•	•	•	•	•	•								M	M	29	H
Librarians	•	•	•	•	•	•		•					•	M	L	16	H
Archivists and curators			•	•	•									M	L	1	H
Health Diagnosing and Treating Practitioners																	
Chiropractors	•	•	•	•	•	•	•							H	H	9	H
Dentists	•	•	•	•	•	•	•							H	H	39	H
Optometrists	•	•	•	•	•	•	•							H	H	8	H
Physicians	•	•	•	•	•	•	•						•	H	H	109	H
Podiatrists	•	•	•	•	•	•	•							H	H	4	H
Veterinarians	•	•	•	•	•	•	•	•	•					H	H	9	H

' Estimates not available.
' Less than 500.

	Job requirements								Work environment				Occupational characteristics			
	1. Leadership/persuasion	2. Helping/instructing others	3. Problem-solving/creativity	4. Initiative	5. Work as part of a team	6. Frequent public contact	7. Manual dexterity	8. Physical stamina	9. Hazardous	10. Outdoors	11. Confined	12. Geographically concentrated	13. Part-time	14. Earnings	15. Employment growth	16. Number of new jobs through 1995 (in thousands)	17. Entry requirements

Registered Nurses, Pharmacists, Dietitians, Therapists, and Physician Assistants

	1	2	3	4	5	6	7	8	9	10	11	12	13	14	15	16	17
Dietitians and nutritionists	●	●	●	●	●	●								M	H	12	H
Occupational therapists	●	●	●	●	●	●	●	●						'	H	8	H
Pharmacists	●	●	●	●	●	●						●		H	L	15	H
Physical therapists	●	●	●	●	●	●	●	●						M	H	25	H
Physician assistants	●	●	●	●	●	●	●							M	H	10	M
Recreational therapists	●	●	●	●	●	●	●	●		●				M	H	4	M
Registered nurses	●	●	●	●	●	●	●	●	●				●	M	H	452	M
Respiratory therapists	●	●	●	●	●	●	●							M	H	11	L
Speech pathologists and audiologists	●	●	●	●	●	●								M	M	8	H

Health Technologists and Technicians

	1	2	3	4	5	6	7	8	9	10	11	12	13	14	15	16	17
Clinical laboratory technologists and technicians		●		●		●					●			L	L	18	'
Dental hygienists		●		●	●	●	●						●	L	H	22	M
Dispensing opticians		●	●	●	●	●								M	H	10	M
Electrocardiograph technicians		●	●		●	●								'	M	3	M
Electroencephalographic technologists and technicians		●	●		●	●								'	H	1	M
Emergency medical technicians	●	●	●	●	●	●	●	●	●	●				L	L	3	M
Licensed practical nurses		●			●	●	●	●					●	L	M	106	M
Medical record technicians						●						●		L	H	10	M
Radiologic technologists		●			●	●	●		●					L	H	27	M
Surgical technicians		●			●	●	●							L	M	5	M

Writers, Artists, and Entertainers

Communications Occupations

	1	2	3	4	5	6	7	8	9	10	11	12	13	14	15	16	17
Public relations specialists	●		●	●	●	●								H	H	30	H
Radio and television announcers and newscasters	●	●		●	●	●						●		L	M	6	H
Reporters and correspondents	●		●	●	●	●								'	M	13	H
Writers and editors	●		●	●	●							●	●	'	H	54	H

Visual Arts Occupations

	1	2	3	4	5	6	7	8	9	10	11	12	13	14	15	16	17
Designers			●	●	●	●	●							H	H	46	H
Graphic and fine artists			●				●								H	60	M
Photographers and camera operators			●	●		●	●						●	M	H	29	M

Performing Arts Occupations

	1	2	3	4	5	6	7	8	9	10	11	12	13	14	15	16	17
Actors, directors, and producers			●	●	●	●	●	●				●	●	L	H	11	M
Dancers and choreographers			●	●	●	●	●	●				●	●	L	H	2	M
Musicians			●	●	●	●	●	●				●	●	L	M	26	M

' Estimates not available.
' Vary, depending on job.

Job requirements / Work environment / Occupational characteristics

Column key:
1. Leadership/persuasion
2. Helping/instructing others
3. Problem-solving/creativity
4. Initiative
5. Work as part of a team
6. Frequent public contact
7. Manual dexterity
8. Physical stamina
9. Hazardous
10. Outdoors
11. Confined
12. Geographically concentrated
13. Part-time
14. Earnings
15. Employment growth
16. Number of new jobs through 1995 (in thousands)
17. Entry requirements

	1	2	3	4	5	6	7	8	9	10	11	12	13	14	15	16	17
Technologists and Technicians Except Health																	
Engineering and Science Technicians																	
Drafters				•		•			•					M	M	39	M
Electrical and electronics technicians		•		•		•								M	H	202	M
Engineering technicians		•		•		•								M	H	90	M
Science technicians		•		•		•								M	M	40	M
Other technicians																	
Air traffic controllers	•	•	•	•		•			•					H	L	²	H
Broadcast technicians		•		•		•			•					M	H	5	M
Computer programmers		•		•					•					H	H	245	H
Legal assistants				¹	•	¹								M	H	51	L
Library technicians		•			•	•	•			•				L	L	4	L
Tool programmers, numerical control		•				•	•							M	H	3	M
Marketing and Sales Occupations																	
Cashiers		•				•	•						•	L	H	566	L
Insurance sales workers	•	•	•	•		•							•	M	L	34	M
Manufacturers' sales workers	•	•	•	•		•								H	L	51	H
Real estate agents and brokers	•	•	•	•		•			•				•	M	M	52	M
Retail sales workers	•	•		•		•							•	L	M	583	L
Securities and financial services sales workers	•	•	•	•		•							•	H	H	32	H
Travel agents	•	•	•	•		•							¹	H	32	M	M
Wholesale trade sales workers	•	•	•	•		•								M	H	369	M
Administrative Support Occupations, Including Clerical																	
Bank tellers						•	•					•	•	L	L	24	L
Bookkeepers and accounting clerks						•						•	•	L	L	118	L
Computer and peripheral equipment operators			•		•							•		L	H	143	M
Data entry keyers						•						•		L	L	10	L
Mail carriers					•	•	•	•		•				M	L	8	L
Postal clerks					•	•	•	•				•		M	L	-27	L
Receptionists and information clerks		•				•	•					•	•	L	M	83	L
Reservation and transportation ticket agents and travel clerks	•	•			•	•						•		M	L	7	L
Secretaries				•	•	•	•					•		L	L	268	L
Statistical clerks						•						•		L	L	-12	L
Stenographers				•	•	•	•							L	L	-96	L
Teacher aides	•	•			•	•	•	•				•	•	L	M	88	L
Telephone operators		•					•					•		L	M	89	L
Traffic, shipping, and receiving clerks				•	•	•								L	L	61	L
Typists							•					•	•	L	L	11	L

¹ Estimates not available.
² Less than 500.

	1. Leadership/persuasion	2. Helping/instructing others	3. Problem-solving/creativity	4. Initiative	5. Work as part of a team	6. Frequent public contact	7. Manual dexterity	8. Physical stamina	9. Hazardous	10. Outdoors	11. Confined	12. Geographically concentrated	13. Part-time	14. Earnings	15. Employment growth	16. Number of new jobs through 1995 (in thousands)	17. Entry requirements
Service Occupations																	
Protective Service Occupations																	
Correction officers	•	•		•		•	•		•					M	H	45	L
Firefighting occupations		•	•		•	•	•	•	•	•			•	M	M	48	L
Guards						•	•	•	•			•	•	L	H	188	L
Police and detectives	•	•	•	•	•	•	•	•	•	•	•			M	M	66	L
Food and Beverage Preparation and Service Occupations																	
Bartenders			•		•	•	•				•		•	L	H	112	M
Chefs and cooks except short order			•			•	•				•		•	L	H	210	M
Waiters and waitresses			•		•	•	•						•	L	H	424	L
Health Service Occupations																	
Dental assistants		•			•	•	•	•					•	L	H	48	L
Medical assistants		•			•	•	•		•					L	H	79	L
Nursing aides		•			•	•	•	•	•				•	L	H	348	L
Psychiatric aides		•			•	•		•	•					L	L	5	L
Cleaning Service Occupations																	
Janitors and cleaners							•						•	L	M	443	L
Personal Service Occupations																	
Barbers					•	•	•				•		•	L	L	4	M
Childcare workers	•	•		•		•		•					•	L	L	55	L
Cosmetologists and related workers					•	•	•	•				•	•	L	H	150	M
Flight attendants		•			•	•	•	•						M	H	13	L
Agricultural, Forestry, and Fishing Occupations																	
Farm operators and managers	•	•	•	•	•		•	•		•				M	L	– 62	L
Mechanics and Repairers																	
Vehicle and Mobile Equipment Mechanics and Repairers																	
Aircraft mechanics and engine specialists			•		•		•	•	•	•		•		H	M	18	M
Automotive and motorcycle mechanics			•		•	•	•	•			•			M	H	185	M
Automotive body repairers			•			•	•	•			•			M	M	32	M
Diesel mechanics			•		•	•	•	•			•			M	H	48	M
Farm equipment mechanics			•			•	•	•	•					M	L	2	M
Mobile heavy equipment mechanics			•			•	•	•			•			M	M	12	M

	Job requirements								Work environment					Occupational characteristics		
	1. Leadership/persuasion	2. Helping/instructing others	3. Problem-solving/creativity	4. Initiative	5. Work as part of a team	6. Frequent public contact	7. Manual dexterity	8. Physical stamina	9. Hazardous	10. Outdoors	11. Confined	12. Geographically concentrated	13. Part-time	14. Earnings	15. Employment growth	16. Number of new jobs through 1995 (in thousands)	17. Entry requirements
Electrical and Electronic Equipment Repairers																	
Commercial and electronic equipment repairers	●	●		●	●									L	M	8	M
Communications equipment mechanics	●	●		●	●									M	L	3	M
Computer service technicians	●	●		●	●									M	H	28	M
Electronic home entertainment equipment repairers	●	●		●	●		●					●		M	M	7	M
Home appliance and power tool repairers	●	●		●	●									L	M	9	M
Line installers and cable splicers	●		●		●	●	●	●						M	M	24	L
Telephone installers and repairers	●		●	●	●	●	●							M	L	−19	L
Other Mechanics and Repairers																	
General maintenance mechanics	●			●			●							M	M	137	M
Heating, air-conditioning, and refrigeration mechanics	●			●			●							M	M	29	M
Industrial machinery repairers	●			●		●	●							M	L	34	M
Millwrights	●			●			●							H	L	6	M
Musical instrument repairers and tuners						●								L	L	1	M
Office machine and cash register servicers	●	●	●		●									M	H	16	M
Vending machine servicers and repairers	●	●			●									'	M	5	M
Construction and Extractive Occupations																	
Construction Occupations																	
Bricklayers and stonemasons	●			●		●	●	●	●					M	M	15	M
Carpenters	●			●		●	●	●	●					M	M	101	M
Carpet installers	●			●	●	●	●	●						M	M	11	M
Concrete masons and terrazzo workers	●			●		●	●	●	●					M	M	17	M
Drywall workers and lathers	●			●		●	●	●						M	M	11	M
Electricians	●			●		●	●	●	●					H	M	88	M
Glaziers	●			●		●	●	●						M	H	8	M
Insulation workers	●			●		●	●	●						M	M	7	M
Painters and paperhangers	●			●	●	●	●	●	●					M	L	17	M
Plasterers	●			●		●	●	●				●		M	L	1	M
Plumbers and pipefitters	●			●	●	●	●	●	●					H	M	61	M
Roofers	●			●		●	●	●	●					L	M	16	M
Sheet-metal workers	●			●		●	●	●						M	M	16	M
Structural and reinforcing metal workers	●			●		●	●	●	●					H	M	16	M
Tilesetters	●			●		●	●							M	M	3	M
Extractive Occupations																	
Roustabouts				●		●	●	●	●			●		M	L	²	L

' Estimates not available.
² Less than 500.

	Job requirements									Work environment				Occupational characteristics			
	1. Leadership/persuasion	2. Helping/instructing others	3. Problem-solving/creativity	4. Initiative	5. Work as part of a team	6. Frequent public contact	7. Manual dexterity	8. Physical stamina	9. Hazardous	10. Outdoors	11. Confined	12. Geographically concentrated	13. Part-time	14. Earnings	15. Employment growth	16. Number of new jobs through 1995 (in thousands)	17. Entry requirements
Production Occupations																	
Blue-collar worker supervisors	●	●	●	●	●		●		●					M	L	85	M
Precision Production Occupations																	
Boilermakers			●			●		●						M	L	4	M
Bookbinding workers		●			●	●	●	●	●					L	M	14	M
Butchers and meatcutters					●	●	●	●	●					L	L	−9	M
Compositors and typesetters						●	●	●	●					L	M	14	M
Dental laboratory technicians							●		●					L	M	10	M
Jewelers	●	●	●	●	●	●	●		●	●				L	L	3	M
Lithographic and photoengraving workers	●	●		●		●	●		●					H	M	13	M
Machinists			●			●	●	●	●					M	L	37	M
Photographic process workers							●		●					L	H	14	L
Shoe and leather workers and repairers		●			●	●	●							L	L	−8	M
Tool-and-die makers			●			●	●	●		●	●			H	L	16	M
Upholsterers						●	●		●					L	L	6	M
Plant and System Operators																	
Stationary engineers			●			●	●	●						M	L	4	M
Water and sewage treatment plant operators			●	●		●		●	●					L	M	10	M
Machine Operators, Tenders, and Setup Workers																	
Metalworking and plastic-working machine operators						●	●	●		●	●				L	3	L
Numerical-control machine-tool operators			●			●	●	●	●					M	H	17	M
Printing press operators	●	●		●		●	●	●	●					M	M	26	M
Fabricators, Assemblers, and Handworking Occupations																	
Precision assemblers					●		●	●	●					L	M	66	L
Transportation equipment painters						●	●	●	●					M	M	9	M
Welders and cutters						●	●	●	●					M	M	41	M
Transportation and Material Moving Occupations																	
Aircraft pilots		●	●	●		●				●				H	H	18	M
Busdrivers		●			●	●	●		●				●	M	M	77	M
Construction machinery operators			●			●	●	●	●	●				M	M	32	M
Industrial truck and tractor operators				●		●	●		●					M	L	−46	M
Truckdrivers				●		●	●		●					M	M	428	M
Handlers, Equipment Cleaners, Helpers, and Laborers																	
Construction trades helpers						●	●	●	●	●				L	L	27	L

individual motivational pattern with the most appropriate jobs. Take, for example, this ideal motivational pattern for a specific sales position with XYZ computer company:

1. Working with technical details
2. Operating in a structured environment where team work is important
3. Using one's ability to plan, initiate new contacts, and follow up

If these are the subject matters, circumstances, abilities, and operating relationships central to your work behavior, then you may be an ideal "fit" for this particular job. While this technique does not use tests and checklists, it does require a great deal of content analysis relevant to the working environments of specific positions. Ideally, this type of analysis should be done on positions within specific organizations. As such, it requires a great deal of investigative work for uncovering the right job for you.

Computer Programs

Several computerized programs provide information on jobs and careers appropriate for people with particular skill and interest profiles. Four of the most popular, comprehensive, and powerful programs are the *Discover II, Sigi-Plus, Job Browser Pro*, and *SkillsUP*. These programs assist users in identifying their skills and interests and then matching them with appropriate jobs. The first two programs are designed for institutional use and thus are extremely expensive to acquire and maintain through yearly fees. The latter two programs are relatively inexpensive and user friendly. We're especially impressed the *Job Browser Pro* which also is available on CD-ROM. This relatively cost-effective program ($295.00) prints out detailed reports on skills and competencies and links them to more than 12,000 occupations. Other relatively inexpensive programs, such as *CareerDesign™, The Right Job Fit™*, and *InterviewSmart™*, are available through the Career Services Group (order online through *www.CareerPerfect.com*).

Most of these programs are widely used in career and counseling centers at community colleges as well as four-year colleges and universities. Even if you are not a student, you should be able to get access to these programs through your local community college. You might also check with your local high school, women's center, or library for information on the availability of these excellent assessment programs. You also can purchase these programs, although most are too expensive for individuals.

Several other computerized job matching programs are also available. In particular, look for the following:

- *Cambridge Career Counseling System*
- *Choices*
- *Computerized Career Information System*
- *Jumpstart Your Job Skills*
- *The Micro Guide to Careers Series*

Conduct Research

We strongly recommend that you conduct research on jobs and organizations related to your MAS and objectives. This research can take different forms, from visiting various employment websites, consulting key directories, and reading books on alternative jobs to interviewing employees and potential employers in particular organizations. Your goal should be to get as much detailed information on jobs and organizations as possible. You want to know how particular jobs and employers relate to your MAS and objectives:

- What types of people (personality, interests, skills) are best suited for each job?

- What type of environment do employees find themselves in?

- What appear to be the major requirements for success in this job?

- How are employees rewarded for their efforts?

- What kinds of relationships are employees expected to establish and maintain?

Answers to these questions will help you determine if particular jobs and organizations are appropriate "fits" given your MAS and objectives.

Your local library should be filled with useful job and career information for initial research. Reference and document rooms of libraries have some of the best career resources. Career planning offices at colleges and universities have a wealth of job and career information in their specialized libraries—a wider selection than most general libraries.

If you use the Internet, be sure to survey some of today's major job sites that can yield a wealth of information on jobs and employers. Many websites provide a wealth of online information and services: job search tips, resume databases, job listings, frequently asked questions, assessment devises, company and employer profiles, and resource centers. One of the best starting points is Margaret Riley Dikel and Frances Roehm's directory to Internet job sites—_The Guide to Internet Job Searching_ (NTC Publishing). Margaret Riley Dikel also maintains her own website, "The Riley Guide," which has evolved into a key reference tool for accessing the most important job and career sites on the Internet. "The Riley Guide" is found through either of these URLs: _www.rileyguide.com_ or _www.dbm.com/jobguide_. Two other excellent guides to key online employment resources include Gerry Crispin and Mark Mehler's _CareerXroads_ and Pam Dixon's _Job Searching Online For Dummies_.

You should start your research by examining several key directories that provide information on alternative jobs and careers:

- _O*NET Dictionary of Occupational Titles_ (U.S. Department of Labor). Replacing the massive _Dictionary of Occupational Titles_ which identified over 13,000 job titles, the _O*NET_ includes over 1,100 job titles. Each job is annotated, organized by major job categories, cross-referenced by industry and title, and includes training, pay, activities, conditions, knowledge, and skills.

- _Occupational Outlook Handbook_ (U.S. Department of Labor). Published biannually, this is the standard sourcebook on over 200 of America's most popular careers. Provides clear descriptions of each job, including working conditions, educational and training requirements, salaries, and future prospects. You also can access the OOH online by going to the U.S. Department of Labor's website: _http://stats.bls.gov/oco/oco1000.htm_

- *Encyclopedia of Careers and Vocational Guidance*, 4 Volumes (J. G. Ferguson Co.). This standard reference examines hundreds of technical and high-tech occupations in addition to the standard career and job fields. Vol 1: *Industry Profiles*; Vol. 2: *Professional Careers*; Vol. 3: *Specific and General Careers*; Vol. 4: *Technicians Careers.*

- *The Guide For Occupational Exploration* (National Forum Foundation). Based on the U.S. Department of Labor research, this guide lists more than 13,000 jobs by occupational cluster, skills required, job title, and industry groups. This is the key book that provides some analytical substance to the *Dictionary of Occupational Titles* and the *Occupational Outlook Handbook.*

You will also find several books that focus on alternative jobs and careers. NTC Publishing, for example, publishes one of the most comprehensive series of books on alternative jobs and careers. Their books now address over 100 different job and career fields. Representative titles in their *"Opportunities in..."* series include:

- *Opportunities in Advertising*
- *Opportunities in Airline Careers*
- *Opportunities in Banking*
- *Opportunities in Business Management*
- *Opportunities in Child Care*
- *Opportunities in Craft Careers*
- *Opportunities in Electrical Trades*
- *Opportunities in Eye Care*
- *Opportunities in Gerontology*
- *Opportunities in Interior Design*
- *Opportunities in Laser Technology*
- *Opportunities in Microelectronics*
- *Opportunities in Pharmacy*
- *Opportunities in Public Relations*
- *Opportunities in Robotics*
- *Opportunities in Sports and Athletics*
- *Opportunities in Telecommunications*

NTC Publishing also publishes two other useful sets of books in a _**"Careers
in..."**_ and a _**"Careers For You"**_ series. The titles in the _**"Careers in..."**_
series consist of

- _**Careers in Accounting**_
- _**Careers in Advertising**_
- _**Careers in Business**_
- _**Careers in Child Care**_
- _**Careers in Communications**_
- _**Careers in Computers**_
- _**Careers in Education**_
- _**Careers in Engineering**_
- _**Careers in Environment**_
- _**Careers in Finance**_
- _**Careers in Government**_
- _**Careers in Health Care**_
- _**Careers in High Tech**_
- _**Careers in Horticulture and Botany**_
- _**Careers in International Business**_
- _**Careers in Journalism**_
- _**Careers in Law**_
- _**Careers in Marketing**_
- _**Careers in Medicine**_
- _**Careers in Science**_
- _**Careers in Social and Rehabilitation Services**_
- _**Careers in Travel, Tourism, and Hospitality**_

Books in the _**"Careers For You"**_ series include:

- _**Careers For Animal Lovers**_
- _**Careers For Bookworms**_
- _**Careers For Born Leaders**_
- _**Careers For Car Buffs**_
- _**Careers For Caring People**_
- _**Careers For Class Clowns & Other Engaging Types**_
- _**Careers For Color Connoisseurs & Other Visual Types**_
- _**Careers For Competitive Spirits & Other Peak Performers**_
- _**Careers For Computer Buffs & Other Technological Types**_

- *Careers For Courageous People*
- *Careers For Crafty People*
- *Careers For Culture Lovers & Other Artsy Types*
- *Careers For Cybersurfers*
- *Careers For Environmental Types*
- *Careers For Extroverts*
- *Careers For Fashion Plates*
- *Careers For Film Buffs*
- *Careers For Financial Mavens & Other Money Movers*
- *Careers For Foreign Language Aficionados*
- *Careers For Geniuses & Other Gifted Types*
- *Careers For Good Samaritans*
- *Careers For Gourmets*
- *Careers For Health Nuts*
- *Careers For High Energy People*
- *Careers For History Buffs*
- *Careers For Homebodies & Other Independent Souls*
- *Careers For Introverts & Other Solitary Types*
- *Careers For Kids at Heart*
- *Careers For Legal Eagles*
- *Careers For Music Lovers*
- *Careers For Mystery Lovers*
- *Careers For Nature Lovers*
- *Careers For Night Owls*
- *Careers For Numbers Crunchers*
- *Careers For Patriotic Types*
- *Careers For Perfectionists & Other Meticulous Types*
- *Careers For Plant Lovers*
- *Careers For Romantics*
- *Careers For Scholars & Other Deep Thinkers*
- *Careers For Self Starters*
- *Careers For Shutterbugs*
- *Careers For Sports Nuts*
- *Careers For the Stagestruck*
- *Careers For Talkative Types*
- *Careers For Travel Buffs*
- *Careers For Writers*

Facts on File publishes seven books on alternative jobs and careers in various industries:

- _**Career Opportunities in Advertising and Public Relations**_
- _**Career Opportunities in Art**_
- _**Career Opportunities in the Food and Beverage Industry**_
- _**Career Opportunities in the Music Industry**_
- _**Career Opportunities in Theater and Performing Arts**_
- _**Career Opportunities in Travel and Tourism**_
- _**Career Opportunities in Writing**_

Several other publishers (Adams, Arco, Ferguson, Peterson's, Impact, IDG, St. Martin) product numerous books on various career fields. If you are unable to find these books in your local library or bookstore, they can be ordered directly from Impact Publications (see order information at the end of this book or through _www.impactpublications.com_).

Target Organizations

After completing research on occupational alternatives, you should identify specific organizations which you are interested in learning more about. Next, compile lists of names, addresses, and telephone numbers of important individuals in each organization. Also, explore the home pages of various organizations on the Internet and write or telephone them for information, such as an annual report and recruiting literature. The most important information you should be gathering concerns the organizations' goals, structures, functions, problems, and projected future opportunities and development. Since you invest part of your life in such organizations, treat them as you would a stock market investment. Compare and evaluate different organizations.

Several directories will assist you in researching organizations. Most are available in the reference sections of libraries; some, such as the Hoover's books, also are available online:

- _**Directory of American Firms Operating in Foreign Countries**_
- _**The Directory of Corporate Affiliations: Who Owns Whom**_
- _**Dun & Bradstreet's Middle Market Directory**_
- _**Dun & Bradstreet's Million Dollar Directory**_

- *Dun & Bradstreet's Reference Book of Corporate Managements*
- *Encyclopedia of Business Information Sources*
- *Fitch's Corporation Reports*
- *Hoover's*
- *MacRae's Blue Book*
- *Moody's Manuals*
- *The Multinational Marketing and Employment Directory*
- *Standard & Poor's Industrial Index*
- *Standard Rate and Data Business Publications Directory*
- *Thomas' Register of American Manufacturers*

Peterson's, along with Hoover's, publishes three annual directories in their *Job Opportunities Series*. These are the definitive guides to organizations that hire business, engineering, computer science, health care, and science graduates:

- *Job Opportunities Business*
- *Job Opportunities Engineering & Computer Science*
- *Job Opportunities Health & Science*

The following trade books identify organizations that are considered to be some of the best to work for today:

- *100 Best Companies to Work For in America*
- *150 Best Companies For Liberal Arts Graduates*
- *America's Fastest Growing Employers*
- *Hidden Job Market*
- *Hoover's Top 2,500 Employers*
- *Job Seekers Guide to 1000 Top Employers*

If you are interested in jobs with a particular organization, you should contact the personnel office for information on the types of jobs offered within the organization. Most companies maintain home pages on the Internet which routinely list job vacancies. You may be able to examine vacancy announcements which describe the duties and responsibilities of specific jobs. If you are interested in working for federal, state, or local governments, each agency will have a personnel office which can supply you with descriptions of their jobs; many also have their own Web pages with details on employment opportunities. While gathering such information, be sure to ask people about their jobs. Four good resources for locating job vacancy announcements include the job finder directories by Dan Lauber (Planning/Communication):

- *Professional's Job Finder*
- *Nonprofit and Education Job Finder*
- *Government Job Finder*
- *International Job Finder*

Contact Individuals

While examining directories and reading books on alternative jobs and careers will provide you with useful job search information, much of this material may be too general for specifying the right job for you. In the end, the best information will come directly from people in specific jobs in specific organizations. To get this information, you must interview people. You especially want to learn more about the people who make the hiring decisions.

You might begin your investigations by contacting various professional and trade associations for detailed information on jobs and careers relevant to their members. For names, addresses, and telephone numbers of such associations, consult the following key directories which are available in most libraries:

- *The Encyclopedia of Associations* (Gale Research)
- *National Trade and Professional Associations* (Columbia Books)

Your most productive research activity will be talking to people. Informal, word-of-mouth communication is still the most effective channel of job search information. In contrast to reading books, people have more current, detailed, and accurate information. Ask them about:

- Occupational fields
- Job requirements and training
- Interpersonal environments
- Performance expectations
- Their problems
- Salaries

- Advancement opportunities
- Future growth potential of the organization
- How best to acquire more information and contacts in a particular field

You may be surprised how willingly friends, acquaintances, and strangers will give you useful information. But before you talk to people, do your library research so that you are better able to ask thoughtful questions.

Network For Information, Advice, and Referrals

As you get further into your job search, networking for information, advice, and referrals will become an important element in your overall job search strategy. At that time you will come into closer contact with potential employers who can provide you with detailed information on their organizations and specific jobs. If you have a well defined MAS, specific job objectives, and a well focused resume, you should be in a good position to make networking pay off with useful information, advice, and referrals. You will quickly discover that the process of linking your MAS and objectives to specific jobs is an ongoing one involving several steps in your job search.

13

Use Time and Plan Effectively

DISCOVERING THE BEST JOBS FOR YOU REQUIRES more than just thinking about what you want to do and completing a battery of self-assessment exercises and tests in the process of conducting a job or career change. You must go far beyond trying to understand who you are and what you want to do. At the very least, you must use your time wisely and develop an effective plan of action that will direct your job search into fruitful areas that lead to job interviews and offers.

When in Doubt, Take Purposeful Action

The old adage *"When in doubt, do something"* is especially relevant when expanded to include a thoughtful plan of action related to the job search process, as outlined in Chapter 4: *"When in doubt, engage in a concrete activity related to the sequence of job search steps."* This might include conducting research on communities, companies, positions, and salaries; surveying job vacancy announcements; writing a resume and job search letters; or contacting three employers each day.

But developing a plan and taking action are much easier said than done. If conducted properly, a job search can become an extremely time consuming activity. It inevitably competes with other personal and professional priorities. That's why you need to make some initial

165

decisions as to how and when you will conduct a job search. How much time, for example, are you willing to set aside each day or week to engage in each of the seven job search activities outlined on page 44? After you've spent numerous hours identifying your abilities and skills and formulating an objective, are you willing to commit yourself to 20 hours a week to network for information and advice? If you are unwilling to commit both your time and yourself to each activity within the process, you may remain stuck, and inevitably frustrated, at the initial stages of self-awareness and understanding. Success only comes to those who take action at other stages in the job search process.

Use Time Wisely

If you decide to conduct your own job search with minimum assistance from professionals, your major cost will be your time. Therefore, you must find sufficient time to devote to your job search. Ask yourself this question:

> *"How valuable is my time in relation to finding a job*
> *or changing my career?"*

Assign a dollar value to your time. For example, is your time worth $3, $5, $10, $25, $50, or $100 an hour? Compare your figure with what you might pay a professional for doing much of the job search work for you. Normal professional fees range from $2,000 to $12,000.

The time you devote to your job search will depend on whether you want to work at it on a full-time or part-time basis. If you are unemployed, by all means make this a full-time endeavor—40 to 80 hours per week. If you are presently employed, we do not recommend quitting your job in order to look for employment. You will probably need the steady income and attendant health benefits during your transition period. Furthermore, it is easier to find new employment by appearing employed. Unemployed people project a negative image in the eyes of many employers—they appear to need a job. *Your goal is to find a job based on your strengths rather than your needs.*

However, if you go back to school for skills retraining, your present employment status may be less relevant to employers. Your major strength is the fact that you have acquired a skill the employer needs. If you quit your job and spend money retraining, you will communicate a certain degree of risk-taking, drive, responsibility, and dedication which employers readily seek, but seldom find, in candidates today.

Assuming you will be conducting a job search on a part-time basis—15 to 25 hours per week—you will need to find the necessary time for engaging in several different job search activities. Unfortunately, most people are too busy to put in the necessary time, having programmed every hour to other "important" personal and professional activities. Thus, conducting a job search for 15 or more hours a week means that some things will have to go or receive low priority in relation to your job search.

This is easier said than done. The job search often gets low priority. It competes with other important daily routines, such as attending meetings, taking children to games, going shopping, watching favorite TV programs, or using the Internet. Rather than fight with your routines—and create family disharmony and stress—make your job search part of your daily routines by improving your overall management of time.

Certain time management techniques will help you make your job search a high-priority activity in your daily schedule. These practices may actually lower your present stress level and thus enhance your overall effectiveness.

Time management experts estimate that most people waste their time on unimportant matters. Lacking priorities, people spend 80 percent of their time on trivia and 20 percent of their time on the important matters which should get the most attention. If you reverse this emphasis, you could have a great deal of excess time—and probably experience less stress attendant with the common practice of crisis-managing the critical 20 percent.

Before reorganizing your time, you must know how you normally use your time. Therefore, complete the exercise on pages 168-169 to assess your time management behavior. While many of these statements are relevant to individuals in managerial positions, respond to those statements that are most relevant to your employment situation. If you answered "no" to many of these statements, you should consider incorporating a few basic time management principles and practices into your daily schedule.

Don't go to extremes by drastically restructuring your life around the "religion" of time management. If you followed all the advice of time management experts, you would probably alienate your family, friends,

Your Time Management Inventory

Respond to each statement by circling "yes" or "no," depending on which response best represents your normal pattern of behavior.

1. I have a written set of long, intermediate, and short-range goals for myself (and my family).   Yes   No

2. I have a clear idea of what I will do today at work and at home.   Yes   No

3. I have a clear idea of what I want to accomplish at work this coming week and month.   Yes   No

4. I set priorities and follow through on the most important tasks first.   Yes   No

5. I judge my success by the results I produce in relation to my goals.   Yes   No

6. I use a daily, weekly, and monthly calendar for scheduling appointments and setting work targets.   Yes   No

7. I delegate as much work as possible.   Yes   No

8. I get my subordinates to organize their time in relation to mine.   Yes   No

9. I file only those things which are essential to my work. When in doubt, I throw it out.   Yes   No

10. I throw away junk mail.   Yes   No

11. My briefcase is uncluttered, including only essential materials; it serves as my office away from the office.   Yes   No

12. I minimize the number of meetings and concentrate on making decisions rather than discussing aimlessly.   Yes   No

13. I make frequent use of the telephone and face-to-face encounters rather than written communications.   Yes   No

14. I make minor decisions quickly.   Yes   No

15. I concentrate on accomplishing one thing at a time.　　Yes　No

16. I handle each piece of paper once and only once.　　Yes　No

17. I answer most letters on the letter I receive with either a handwritten or typed message.　　Yes　No

18. I set deadlines for myself and others and follow through in meeting them.　　Yes　No

19. I reserve time each week to plan.　　Yes　No

20. My desk and work area are well organized and clear.　　Yes　No

21. I know how to say "no" and do so.　　Yes　No

22. I first skim books, articles, and other forms of written communication for ideas before reading further.　　Yes　No

23. I monitor my time use during the day by asking myself "How can I best use my time at present?"　　Yes　No

24. I deal with the present by getting things done that need to be done.　　Yes　No

25. I maintain a time log to monitor the best use of my time.　　Yes　No

26. I place a dollar value on my time and behave accordingly.　　Yes　No

27. I—not others—control my time.　　Yes　No

28. My briefcase includes items I can work on during spare time in waiting rooms, lines, and airports.　　Yes　No

29. I keep my door shut when I'm working.　　Yes　No

30. I regularly evaluate to what degree I am achieving my stated goals.　　Yes　No

and colleagues with your narrow efficiency mentality! A realistic approach is to start monitoring your time use and then gradually re-organize your time according to goals and priorities. This is all you need to do. Forget the elaborate flow charts that are the stuff of expensive time management workshops and consultants. Start by developing a time management log that helps you monitor your present use of time. Keep daily records of how you use your time over a two-week period. Identify who controls your time and the results of your time utilization. Within two weeks, clear patterns will emerge. You may learn that you have an "open door" policy that enables others to control your time, leaving little time to do your own work. Based on this information, you may need to close your door and be more selective about access. You may find from your analysis that you use most time for activities that have few if any important outcomes. If this is the case, then you may need to set goals and prioritize daily activities.

A simple yet effective technique for improving your time management practices is to complete a "to do" list for each day. You can purchase tablets of these forms in many stationery and office supply stores, or you can develop your own "Things To Do Today" list. This list also should prioritize which activities are most important to accomplish each day. Include at the top of your list a particular job search activity or several activities that should be completed on each day. If you follow this simple time management practice, you will find the necessary time to include your job search in your daily routines. You can give your job search top priority. Better still, you will accomplish more in less time, and with better results.

Plan to Take Action

While we recommend that you plan your job search, we also caution you to avoid the excesses of too much planning. Like time management, planning should not be all-consuming. Planning makes sense because it focuses attention and directs action toward specific goals and targets. It requires you to set goals and develop strategies for achieving the goals. However, too much planning can blind you to unexpected occurrences and opportunities—that wonderful experience called serendipity. Given the highly decentralized and chaotic nature of the job market, you want to do just enough planning so you will be in a position to take advantage of what will inevitably be unexpected occurrences and opportunities arising from your planned job search activities. Therefore, as you plan your job search, be sure you are flexible enough to take advantage of new opportunities.

Based on our previous discussion of the sequence of job search steps, we outline on page 172 a hypothetical plan for conducting an effective job search. This plan incorporates the individual job search activities (Chapter 4) over a six-month period. If you phase in the first five job search steps during the initial three to four weeks and continue the final four steps in subsequent weeks and months, you should begin receiving job offers within two to three months after initiating your job search. Interviews and job offers can come anytime—often unexpectedly—as you conduct your job search. An average time is three months, but it can occur within a week or take as long as five months. If you plan, prepare, and persist at the job search, the pay-off will be job interviews and offers.

Job hunting requires time and hard work. If done properly, it can pay off with a job that is right for you.

While three months may seem a long time, especially if you have just lost your job and you need work immediately, you can shorten your job search time by increasing the frequency of your individual job search activities. If you are job hunting on a full-time basis, you may be able to cut your job search time in half. But don't expect to get a job—especially a job that's right for you—within a week or two. Job hunting requires time and hard work—perhaps the hardest work you will ever do—but if done properly, it can pay off with a job that is right for you.

Organization of Job Search Activities

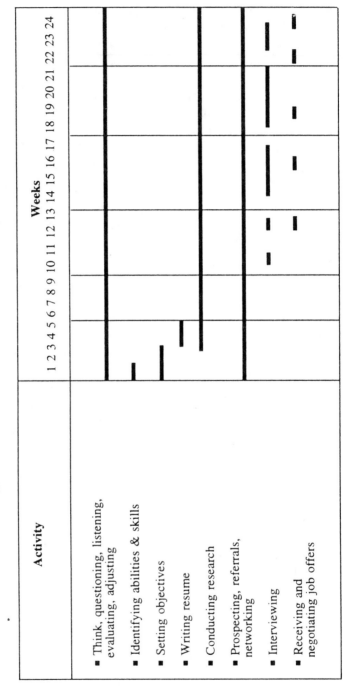

14

Develop Strategies
For Success

SUCCESS IS DETERMINED BY MORE THAN JUST A GOOD plan getting implemented. We know success is not determined primarily by intelligence, time management, or luck. Success in conducting a job search involves a lot more than following certain steps, such as doing a self-assessment, formulating an objective, or writing resumes and letters. Based upon experience, theory, research, common sense, and acceptance of some self-transformation principles, we believe you will achieve job search success by following most of these 21 principles:

1. **You should work hard at finding a job:** Make this a daily endeavor and involve your family. Focus on managing the specific details of your job search.

2. **You should not be discouraged with set-backs:** You are playing the odds, so expect disappointments and handle them in stride. You will get many "no's" before finding the one "yes" which is right for you. Indeed, rejections should be expected and accepted as part of the game.

3. **You should be patient and persevere:** Expect three to six months of hard work before you connect with the job that's

right for you. If you give up prematurely, after only a few rejections, you may miss out on some great opportunities had you been more patient and persevered.

4. **You should use multiple approaches to finding the right job for you.** There is no one best way to find a job. While interpersonal networking pays off for many job seekers, so does responding to classified ads, using resume databases, and responding to opportunities on the Internet.

5. **You should be honest with yourself and others:** Honesty is always the best policy. But don't be naive and stupid by confessing your negatives and shortcomings to others.

6. **You should develop a positive attitude toward yourself:** Nobody wants to employ guilt-ridden people with inferiority complexes. Focus on your positive characteristics.

7. **You should associate with positive and successful people:** Finding a job largely depends on how well you relate to others. Avoid associating with negative people who complain and have a "you-can't-do-it" attitude. Run with winners who have a positive "can-do" outlook on life.

8. **You should set goals:** You should have a clear idea of what you want and where you are going. Without these, you will present a confusing and indecisive image to others. Clear goals help direct your job search into productive channels. Moreover, setting high goals will help make you work hard in getting what you want.

9. **You should plan:** Convert your goals into action steps that are organized as short-, intermediate-, and long-range plans.

10. **You should get organized:** Translate your plans into activities, targets, names, addresses, telephone numbers, email addresses, and materials. Develop an efficient and effective filing system and use a calendar to set time targets, record appointments, and compile useful information.

11. **You should be a good communicator:** Take stock of your oral, written, and nonverbal communication skills. How well do you communicate? Since most aspects of your job search involve communicating with others, and communication skills are one of the most sought-after skills, always present yourself well both verbally and nonverbally.

12. **You should be energetic and enthusiastic:** Employers are attracted to positive people. They don't like negative and depressing people who toil at their work. Generate enthusiasm both verbally and nonverbally. Check on your telephone voice—it may be more unenthusiastic than your voice in face-to-face situations.

13. **You should ask questions:** Your best information comes from asking questions. Learn to develop intelligent questions that are non-aggressive, polite, and interesting to others. But don't ask too many questions and thereby become a bore or labeled as a potential employee who "talks too much!"

14. **You should be a good listener:** Being a good listener is often more important than being a good questioner or talker. Learn to improve your face-to-face listening behavior (nonverbal cues) as well as remember and use information gained from others. Make others feel they enjoyed talking with you, i.e., you are one of the few people who actually *listen* to what they say.

15. **You should be polite, courteous, and thoughtful:** Treat gatekeepers, especially receptionists and secretaries, like human beings. Avoid being aggressive or too assertive. Try to be polite, courteous, and gracious. Your social graces are being observed. Remember to send thank-you letters—a very thoughtful thing to do in a job search. Even if rejected, thank employers for the "opportunity" given to you. After all, they may later have additional opportunities, and they will remember you.

16. **You should be tactful:** Watch what you say to others about other people and your background. Don't be a gossip, backstabber, or confessor.

17. **You should maintain a professional stance:** Be neat in what you do and wear, and speak with the confidence, authority, and maturity of a professional.

18. **You should demonstrate your intelligence and competence by focusing on your accomplishments:** Present yourself as someone who gets things done and achieves results—a *producer.* Employers generally seek people who are bright, hard working, responsible, communicate well, have positive personalities, maintain good interpersonal relations, are likable, observe dress and social codes, take initiative, are talented, possess expertise in particular areas, use good judgment, are cooperative, trustworthy, and loyal, generate confidence and credibility, and are conventional. In other words, they like people who score in the "excellent" to "outstanding" categories of their performance evaluation.

19. **You should not overdo your job search:** Don't engage in overkill and bore everyone with your "job search" stories. Achieve balance in everything you do. Occasionally take a few days off to do nothing related to your job search. Develop a system of incentives and rewards—such as two non-job search days a week, if you accomplish targets A, B, C, and D.

20. **You should be open-minded and keep an eye open for "luck":** Too much planning can blind you to unexpected and fruitful opportunities. You should welcome serendipity. Learn to re-evaluate your goals and strategies. Seize new opportunities if they appear appropriate.

21. **You should evaluate your progress and adjust:** Take two hours once every two weeks and evaluate what you are doing and accomplishing. If necessary, tinker with your plans and reorganize your activities and priorities. Don't become too routinized and thereby kill creativity and innovation.

15

Online Career
Assessment Resources

THROUGHOUT THIS BOOK WE HAVE RECOMMENDED several resources that can assist you in discovering the right job for you. Many of these resources are in the form of books, tests, and software. Others, as we outlined in Chapter 5, are career professionals who offer numerous career planning and job search services. At the same time, we've made reference to a few key websites.

In this final chapter, we review several online resources which are available to assist job seekers with the critical assessment stage of their job search. You should visit several of these websites for more information on their particular inventories and services. Many of them offer free online tests, whereas others charge a fee for taking an online test, receiving a detailed report, and/or consulting a career professional.

Online Career Resources

Within the past five years, the traditional job search has been enhanced through the growth of many Internet employment sites, as you can quickly see by visiting Margaret Riley Dikel's gateway site to job finding on the Internet: *www.rileyguide.com*. Some are large integrated sites complete with resume databases, job listings, employer profiles, career news, job search articles and tips, message boards, career advisors, salary calculators, frequently asked questions (FAQs), and interactive assessment inventories and tests. Other sites are more specialized, focusing on one particular dimension of the job search, such as researching employers, job listings, headhunters, resumes, interviewing, salary negotiations, or assessment. If you're using the Internet in your job search, you definitely should be connected to several of these major websites:

Monster.com:	*www.monster.com*
CareerBuilder:	*www.careerbuilder.com*
	www.careerpath.com
NationJob:	*www.nationjob.com*
FlipDog:	*www.flipdog.com*
Hot Jobs:	*www.hotjobs.com*
Vault.com:	*www.vault.com*
VirtualResume:	*www.virtualresume.com*
Headhunter.net:	*www.headhunter.net*
	www.careermosaic.com
America's Job Bank:	*www.ajb.com*
CareerWeb:	*www.careerweb.com*
Career Journal:	*www.careerjournal.com*
Dice:	*www.dice.com*
Employment911.com:	*www.employment911.com*
WebFeet.com:	*www.webfeet.com*
PlanetRecruit:	*www.planetrecruit.com*
Career.com:	*www.career.com*
6FigureJobs.com:	*www.6figurejobs.com*
4Work:	*www.4work.com*
BestJobsUSA:	*www.bestjobsusa.com*
BrilliantPeople.com:	*www.brilliantpeople.com*
Career City:	*www.careercity.com*
JobOptions:	*www.joboptions.com*
JobTrak:	*www.jobtrak.com*
CampusCareerCenter:	*www.campuscareercenter.com*
HireAbility:	*www.hireability.com*
HireStrategy:	*www.hirestrategy.com*
WashingtonJobs:	*www.washingtonjobs.com*
JobStar:	*www.jobstar.org*

If you are interested in auctioning your talents, especially on a freelance basis, check out these novel job auction sites:

Monster.com:	*www.talentmarket.monster.com*
FreeAgent:	*www.freeagent.com*
Bid4Geeks:	*www.bid4geeks.com*
Ants.com:	*www.ants.com*
eLance.com:	*www.elance.com*

While some of these websites include interactive career assessment devices, other sites are more specialized in dealing with various aspects of career assessment. As you explore these sites, we caution you in using many of these online resources. There is nothing magical about these online assessment tools. Many are useful in providing information on your personality and career interests, preferences, and values, but they are not necessarily good predictors of career choice and satisfaction. In fact, many of the self-directed exercises outlined in this book may be more useful. In the end, you are well advised to contact a career professional who can administer the best tests and interpret the results for you. This is especially true in the case of the three most popular assessment devices used in career counseling and which are not available in complete form on the Internet:

> *There is nothing magical about these online tools. In the end, you are well advised to contact a career professional.*

- *Myers-Briggs Type Indicator*
- *Strong Interest Inventory*
- *Self-Directed Search*

All three require the assistance of a career professional to both administer the inventories and interpret the results. It's the *interpretation* that is so important and which requires the assistance of a trained career professional.

Online Inventories and Tests

The following websites offer a wide variety of assessment inventories and tests to assist you with your career planning. Focusing primarily on personality types and decision-making styles, few of these devices actually deal directly with career choices. Many, however, do relate results to specific jobs or careers by indicating the individual might find a particular cluster of jobs and careers enjoyable given his or her particular personality and temperament type. Most online tests are free, whereas others provide an introduction to or sample of the particular device which will require payment; the most expensive services also require consultation, usually by phone, with a career professional.

Taking these tests can be a very seductive experience. As we noted earlier, many such tests result in the *"aha"* effect—they tell you the obvious but have little influence on your future behavior. Others are just fun to take and result in useful self-discovery information which may influence your career choices. Overall, we recommend taking several different tests. Each one may yield useful information and several of them may validate similar results. Above all, we recommend contacting a certified career counselor to help interpret results as well as administer more detailed assessment inventories. These three websites include contact information on hundreds of certified career counselors worldwide:

> *www.nbcc.org*
> *http://ncda.org*
> *www.CertifiedCareerCoaches.com*

In addition in meeting with them for private consultation, many of these counselors will consult with you by telephone or over the Internet.

JobHuntersBible	**Job Search Advice**
www.jobhuntersbible.com	**Free**

This is the website of job search guru Richard Bolles, the author of the phenomenal bestselling career guide, **What Color Is Your Parachute?** While the site is filled with lots of useful career planning and job search advice, it includes a section on "Tests and Advice" with linkages to several websites offering online career tests and personality inventories. Includes useful advice, and cautionary notes, on taking such tests and relating them to your own career choices.

CareerHub	Myers-Briggs Type Indicator
www.careerhub.org	Counselor assisted

This is the closest you'll get to an online version of the *Myers-Briggs Type Indicator*—a sample test with interpretation. Operated by Consulting Psychologists Press (*www.cpp-db.com*), which has proprietary rights to the *Myers-Briggs Type Indicator, Strong Interest Inventory*, and the *Skills Confidence Inventory*, the site provides useful information on the career planning process, explains the various devices, and includes linkages to career professionals (through the National Board of Certified Counselors, *www.nbcc.org*) who are certified to administer the various inventories and tests produced by this company. This site also is linked to the publisher's relatively new online training website, *www.SkillsOne.com*.

Keirsey Character Sorter and	Questionnaires
Keirsey Temperament Sorter	Information
www.keirsey.com	Free

Based on the Myers-Briggs Type Indicator and Dr. Kersey's bestselling books, *Please Understand Me* and *Please Understand Me II*, the Keirsey temperament approach classifies individuals into four temperaments: Guardian, Artisan, Idealist, Rational. This site provides lots of information on these two assessment devices, contrasting them with what they consider to be the less stable results of the Myers-Briggs Type Indicator. Offers online questionnaires for taking the tests in English, Spanish, Portuguese, German, Norwegian, Swedish, Bosnian, Czech, and Danish.

U.S. Department of Interior	MBTI Career Chart
www.doi.gov/octc/typescar.html	Free

For a good example of how the Myers-Briggs Type Indicator relates to specific jobs and careers (without having to take the test) visit this useful page which includes 16 personality types with corresponding jobs and careers linked to each. If, for example, you are an ISTJ type, chances are you will enjoy being an engineer, stock broker, police officer, or real estate agent.

PersonalityType	Quiz
www.personalitytype.com	Free

This is the website of psychologists and bestselling authors Paul D. Tieger and Barbara Barron-Tieger (*Do What You Are*, *Nurture By Nature*, *The Art of Speedreading People*, and *Just Your Type*). Using the popular personality type approach (based on the Myers-Briggs Type Indicator and a whole school of "Type" psychologists who provide answers to all kinds of life challenges through their analyses), they offer an online quiz to help you identify your "Type." They claim this information will help you better deal with your career, love life, parenting skills, and communication with others. The site includes linkages to professional organizations and Type experts as well as FAQs, a store, and their books.

Personality Online	Tests
www.spods.net/personality	Free

This inviting site will really help you probe various dimensions of your personality. It includes nine self-scoring personality tests as well as information on analysis and resources relating to personal development. Several of the tests have implications for career decision-making: Keisey Temperament Sorter, The Enneagram, Personality Profile, The Geek Test, The Nerd Test, and the Maykorner Test. The site also includes a few fun tests: The Love Test, The Colour Test, and The Purity Test. The site is especially noted for The Enneagram, a popular self-discovery device, which measures personality along nine different scales and which are linked to several personality traits; it includes 180 questions and results in classifying the user into nine different types: Perfectionist, Giver, Performer, Tragic Romantic, Observer, Devil's Advocate, Epicure, Boss, and Mediator (for more information on the Enneagram, visit *www.ennea.com*). The 80-statement Personality Profile measures users on 14 different profiles or "types" which are related to several personality traits.

Self-Directed Search	**Test**
www.self-directed-search.com	**$8.95**

Self-Directed Search (*www.self-directed-search.com*): This is the home site for John Holland's popular *Self-Directed Search (SDS)* which is used by millions of students and job seekers each year. The SDS classifies individuals into six categories: Realistic, Investigative, Artistic, Social, Enterprising, and Conventional. A proprietary self-assessment device produced by Psychological Assessment Resources (PAR), the SDS has influenced the thinking of many career counselors and is the basis for much of Richard Bolles's self-assessment devices, including his popular *Quick Job Hunting Map*. This site explains the SDS and provides an example of an SDS report for someone with an ESC Holland code. Visitors to this site can take an online version of the SDS and have the results printed out (8-12 page report) for $8.95 (takes credit cards online). The site also includes information on selecting a career counselor, along with linkages to the National Career Development Association (*http://ncda.org*) and the National Board of Certified Counselors (*www.nbcc.org*).

Birkman Method	**Quiz**
Princeton Review Career Quiz	**Free**
www.review.com/career/article.cfm?id=career/car_quiz_intro	

This 24-question quiz is designed to help users determine their most likely interests and work style for making better career choices. After registering and taking this free online quiz, you receive lots of information on jobs and careers relating to the analysis of your answers. Much of the same information is found in the book, *The Princeton Review Guide to Your Career*.

Career Services Group *www.careerperfect.com*	**Software** **Purchase**

Offers information and advice on various types of career inventories and tests: career interest, values, skills, and personality. Includes a self-scored "Work Preference Inventory." Also includes three software programs which can be purchased through the site's store: *CareerDesign* ($49.95), *The Right Job Fit* ($34.95), and *InterviewSmart* ($9.95).

QueenDom *www.queendom.com*	**Tests** **Free**

Test junkies will enjoy exploring this site. It includes numerous personality, intelligence, and health-related tests and questionnaires. "Test junkie" section includes linkages to several career-related tests on the Internet.

Personality and IQ Tests *www.davideck.com*	**Gateway Site** **Free**

This site is jam-packed with linkages to a variety of personality, IQ, love, health, career, and other fun tests. Each test is rated on a scale of 0 to 4. The personality test section includes the IPIP-NEO (competitor to the Myers-Briggs Type Indicator), Enneagram, Quizbox.com Personality, Luscher Colour, Kingdomality Personality, Keirsey Temperament, Keirsey Temperament Sorter II, MayKorner Personality, Goofy Personality, and more than 20 other tests. The career test section includes the Microsoft Online Skills Assessment (for fitting into the IT industry), Typing Test, Are You a Risk Taker?, Situation Maker or Taker?, The Entrepreneur Test, Panhandling Effectiveness Survey, Birkman Method Career Style Summary, and The Career Key.

Tests on the Web	Gateway Site
www.2h.com	Free & Fee

This bare-bones site includes a variety of IQ, personality, and entrepreneurial tests found on the World Wide Web. The tests are listed by title and accompanied by a short description and the amount of time to complete each one. The personality test section includes 23 tests, including PROFILER, Keirsey Temperament Sorter, VALS, Kingdomality, Power Test, Stress-O-Meter, Life Style Test, Type A Personality Test, Communication Skills, The MayKorner Personality Test, Self-esteem Test, Anxiety Test, Balance Test, and Are You Assertive?

Fortune.com	Quizzes
www.fortune.com/careers/	Free

Fortune Magazine's website offers eight free quizzes for employees and job seekers:

- *What's Your Ideal Career?*
- *How High Is Your Work EQ?*
- *Are Your Employees Ready to Change?*
- *Do You Deserve a Raise?*
- *Will You Be Promoted Soon?*
- *Is It Time to Switch Jobs?*
- *What's Your Charisma Quotient?*
- *Do You Have a Fear of Success?*

Profiler	CISS®
www.profiler.com	$17.95

The CISS (Campbell™ Interest and Skill Survey) online assessment is designed to help job seekers discover their right fit in the world of work. The CISS report compares test results with people who are successfully employed in the same fields. Costing $17.95, the personalized report covers nearly 60 occupations and includes a comprehensive career planner for interpreting results.

CareerLab.com	Exercises
www.careerlab.com	Free

Operated by career advisor and author William S. Frank, this site includes a lengthy paper and pencil self-discovery exercise on "How to Create Your Career Blueprint or Vision." The exercise is divided into three parts:

- Likes and Dislikes
- Career Blueprint
- Ideal First Month

The "Testing and Assessment" section of this site includes several instruments which can be purchased online and include 30 minutes to two hours of personal consultation:

- *Campbell Interest and Skill Survey (CISS)*
- *Strong Interest Inventory*
- *Myers-Briggs Type Indicator (MBTI)*
- *Myers-Briggs Type Indicator - Step II*
- *16-Personality Factors Profile*
- *FIRO-B*
- *California Psychological Inventory (CPI)*
- *The Birkman Method*
- *Campbell Leadership Index*

This section of the site includes good descriptions of each instrument, especially the use of the highly respected Birkman Method.

Career Questionnaire	Test
www.collegeboard.org	Free
(http://cbweb9p.collegeboard.org/career/html/searchQues.html)	

Presented by the College Board, this questionnaire helps users find careers that match their interests and abilities. The questionnaire includes 34 questions dealing with temperaments, abilities, working conditions, education, interest areas, salary requirements, and employment outlook.

CareerLeader™   Inventory
www.careerdiscovery.com/careerleader   **$95.00**

CareerLeader™ is a comprehensive business career development tool designed to help individuals discover their best career in business. Developed by Drs. James Waldroop and Timothy Butler, directors of MBA Career Development Programs at Harvard Business School, it's an interactive, online program used by over 120 top business and MBA programs in the US and Europe to help guide students and help companies retain employees. It includes three tests that focus on business-relevant interests, values, and abilities to help individuals with their business careers. The resulting profiles recommend the best career path matches. Comes with a full money-back guarantee within seven days of purchase.

Careers By Design®   Inventories
www.careers-by-design.com   Fees

This company offers four popular assessment devices online followed by telephone counseling sessions for interpreting results:

- *Strong Interest Inventory (SII)*
- *Myers-Briggs Type Indicator (MBTI)*
- *FIRO-B™*
- *The 16 Personality Factors Questionnaire*

Since the site does not reveal prices for these instruments and consultation services, you'll need to call (562-424-0527) this company for pricing information.

Career Interests Game   Free exercise
http://web.missouri.edu/~cppcwww/holland.shtml

Based on Dr. John Holland's *Self-Directed Search*, this quick and easy game is designed to demonstrate how different interests and skills might best relate to various career areas as well as programs of study at the University of Missouri. A very clever use of the SDS which illuminates its many appealing features.

| The Career Key | Exercise |
| www.ncsu.edu/careerkey | Free |

This site is developed as a free public service through the College of Education at North Carolina State University. Using Dr. John Holland's *Self-Directed Search*, the site is designed to help users make better career decisions through self-assessment. Includes online exercises.

Futurestep	Profile
www.futurestep.com	Free sample
(www.futurestep.com/cndt12/sign_in/sample_main.asp)	

This site is operated by the executive recruiting firm of Korn/Ferry International and the *Wall Street Journal*. It includes sample results from two assessment devices used by this company:

- *Career Style Feedback*
- *Desired Job Characteristics*

| GSIA Carnegie Mellon | Free exercise |
| www.gsia.cmu.edu/afs/andrew/gsia/coc/student/assess.html | |

Developed for students in the Graduate School of Industrial Administration (GSIA) at Carnegie Mellon University, this is a paper and pencil self-assessment exercise that generates a great deal of information on the individuals. It asks such questions as *"Describe yourself in one sentence," "What challenges you the most?," "How have you set yourself apart from the crowd?,"* and *"What are the 10 most important things you are looking for in a job?"* Includes a link to the CareerLeader program at Harvard University (*www.careerdiscovery.com*).

| **Interest Finder Quiz** | **Quiz** |
| *www.myfuture.com/career/interest.html* | **Free sample** |

This online quiz helps users decide whether to go to college or look for a job and what are the best jobs for them. Includes a checklist of 60 "like" items which are scored. Analyzes answers and assigns the test taker to two of six work groups related to Dr. John Holland's SDS: Realistic, Investigative, Artistic, Social, Enterprising, or Conventional.

| **The Highlands Program** | **Quizzes** |
| *www.highlandsprogram.com* | **Free** |

Includes three online interactive career and life planning quizzes that deal with several important career questions:

- *Are You a Victim of the Lemming Conspiracy?*
- *How Big is Your Vision?*
- *How Satisfied Are You At Work?*

| **Jackson Vocational Interest Survey** | **Profile** |
| *http://jvis.com/take.htm* | **$14.95** |

This site enables visitors to take an online version of the Jackson Vocational Interest Survey. The survey provides a detailed picture of an individual's career interests. It includes 289 pairs of job-related activities. The cost includes a detailed report showing your career interest patterns with related matching occupations.

| **Emotional Intelligence Quotient** | **Test** |
| *www.utne.com/azEq2.tmpl* | **Free** |

Daniel Goleman's book, *Emotional Intelligence: Why It Can Matter More Than IQ for Character, Health, and Lifelong Achievement*, is the basis for this self-scoring instrument. Includes 10 multiple choice questions which yield a score that is translated into your emotional quotient.

Inner Self Personality Test	Test
www1.wiwo.nl/innerself	Free

This 60-question test, which takes about 20 minutes to complete, is designed for those who want to improve their life by better understanding their personality. Includes one question per screen. Generates an online score. Yields an abbreviated and extensive analysis of one's personality.

Personality Type Test	Test
http://jvis.com/take.htm	Free

This site includes a 52-question test (forced choices) for assessing your personality type based on the work of famous psychologist C. G. Jung, whose personality types theory is the basis for several popular inventories such as the *Myers-Briggs Type Indicator*. It takes about 20 minutes to complete the test and receive an online score that indicates your personality type.

Quick Personality Test	Test
http://users.rcn.com/zang.interport/personality.html	Free

It doesn't get much quicker than this form and color test—just click onto the most appealing of 9 shapes. The results sound very similar to your daily horoscope, which may actually yield better results!

Index

The Authors

RON AND CARYL KRANNICH, PH.Ds, ARE TWO OF America's leading career and travel writers who have authored more than 50 books. A former Peace Corps Volunteer and Fulbright Scholar, Ron received his Ph.D. in Political Science from Northern Illinois University. Caryl received her Ph.D. in Speech Communication from Penn State University. They operate Development Concepts Incorporated, a training, consulting, and publishing firm.

Ron and Caryl are both former university professors, high school teachers, management trainers, and consultants. As trainers and consultants, they have completed numerous projects on management, career development, local government, population planning, and rural development in the United States and abroad.

The Krannichs' career books focus on key job search skills, military and civilian career transitions, government and international careers, travel jobs, and nonprofit organizations. Their body of work represents one of today's most comprehensive collections of career writing. Their books are widely available in bookstores, libraries, and career centers.

Authors of 19 travel-shopping guidebooks on various destinations around the world, Ron and Caryl continue to pursue their international and travel interests through their innovative *Treasures and Pleasures of . . . Best of the Best* travel-shopping series and related website: *www.ishoparoundtheworld.com*. When not found at their home and business in Virginia, they are probably somewhere in Europe, Asia, Africa, the Middle East, the South Pacific, or the Caribbean and South America pursuing their other passion—researching and writing about quality arts and antiques.

As both career and travel experts, the Krannichs' work is frequently featured in major newspapers, magazines, and newsletters as well as on radio, television, and the Internet. They can be contacted through the publisher: *krannich@impactpublications.com*.

Career Resources

THE FOLLOWING CAREER RESOURCES, MANY OF WHICH were mentioned in previous chapters, are available directly from Impact Publications. Complete the following form or list the titles, include postage (see formula at the end), enclose payment, and send your order to:

IMPACT PUBLICATIONS
9104 Manassas Drive, Suite N
Manassas Park, VA 20111-5211
1-800-361-1055 (orders only)
Tel. 703/361-7300 or Fax 703/335-9486
E-mail address: *orders@impactpublications.com*
Quick & easy online ordering: *www.impactpublications.com*

Orders from individuals must be prepaid by check, moneyorder, Visa, MasterCard, or American Express. We accept telephone and fax orders.

Qty.	TITLES	Price	TOTAL

Assessment

Qty.	TITLES	Price	TOTAL
___	Career Satisfaction and Success	14.95	___
___	Career Tests	12.95	___
___	Dictionary of Holland Occupational Codes	49.00	___
___	**Discover the Best Jobs For You**	15.95	___
___	Discover What You're Best At	12.00	___
___	Do What You Are	16.95	___
___	Finding Your Perfect Work	16.95	___
___	Gifts Differing	14.95	___
___	I Could Do Anything If Only I Knew What It Was	12.95	___
___	Making Vocational Choices	29.95	___
___	Real People, Real Jobs	15.95	___
___	Type Talk	11.95	___
___	WORKTypes	12.99	___

Other Great Career Resources

Qty.	TITLES	Price	TOTAL
___	100 Great Jobs and How to Get Them	17.95	___
___	100 Top Internet Job Sites	12.95	___
___	101 Dynamite Answers to Interview Questions	12.95	___
___	101 Dynamite Questions to Ask At Your Job Interview	14.95	___

___	1500+ KeyWords For $100,000+ Jobs	14.95	___
___	Best Jobs For the 21st Century	19.95	___
___	Change Your Job, Change Your Life	17.95	___
___	Complete Guide to Occupational Exploration	39.95	___
___	Dressing Smart For the New Millennium	15.95	___
___	Dynamite Cover Letters	14.95	___
___	Dynamite Resumes	14.95	___
___	Dynamite Salary Negotiations	15.95	___
___	Enhanced Guide For Occupational Exploration	34.95	___
___	Enhanced Occupational Outlook Handbook	37.95	___
___	Get a Raise in 7 Days	14.95	___
___	Haldane's Best Answers to Tough Interview Questions	14.95	___
___	Haldane's Best Cover Letters For Professionals	15.95	___
___	Haldane's Best Resumes For Professionals	15.95	___
___	High Impact Resumes & Letters	19.95	___
___	International Jobs Directory	19.95	___
___	Interview For Success	15.95	___
___	Jobs and Careers With Nonprofit Organizations	17.95	___
___	Jobs For People Who Love to Travel	15.95	___
___	Occupational Outlook Handbook	23.95	___
___	O*NET Dictionary of Occupational Titles	49.95	___
___	Proof of Performance	17.95	___
___	Savvy Interviewer	10.95	___
___	The Savvy Networker	14.95	___
___	What Color Is Your Parachute?	16.95	___

SUBTOTAL ___

Virginia residents add 4½% sales tax ___

POSTAGE/HANDLING ($5 for first
product and 8% of SUBTOTAL over $30) $5.00

8% of SUBTOTAL over $30 -------------------------- ___

TOTAL ENCLOSED ---------------------- ___

NAME _____

ADDRESS _____

_____

_____

❑ I enclose check/moneyorder for $ _____ made payable to
IMPACT PUBLICATIONS.

❑ Please charge $ _____ to my credit card:
  ❑ Visa   ❑ MasterCard   ❑ American Express   ❑ Discover
  Card # _____

  Expiration date: _____/_____
  Signature _____